FERRANTI

Synchronous Electric Clocks

1932-1957

Mark Andrew Lines

Acknowledgements

The Ferranti Collections Department at the Museum of Science and Industry (MOSI) Manchester

Smiths Domestic Clocks - Barrie Smith

Ferranti A History - John F Wilson

Concentration in British Industry - Evely and Little

Publication

Published by:

zazzoo media
23 Hendrix Drive, Crownhill
Milton Keynes, MK8 0DX, UK
www.zazzoo.co.uk info@zazzoo.co.uk

ISBN: 978-0-9572172-0-1 (Paperback) Date of Publication: April 2012
ISBN: 978-0-9572172-1-8 (Hardback) Date of Publication: April 2012

Printed in the UK by: Lightningsource

British Library Cataloguing in Publication Data.
A catalogue record for this book is available from the British Library.

mosi

Museum of Science & Industry

The Ferranti Collection at MOSI

MOSI holds the Ferranti Collection, which comprises the Ferranti company archive and over 1,400 objects from the period 1882 to 1993, when the company ceased trading. The archives include minute books, photographs, technical and commercial records, and private papers belonging to Sebastian Ziani de Ferranti, the original founder of the company. The objects include computers, generating equipment, navigation and defence systems, and domestic appliances, including clocks.

Information about the Ferranti Collection can be accessed through the Collections Online and Ferranti Online facilities via the MOSI website:

http://www.mosi.org.uk/collections/explore-the-collections.aspx

Researchers wishing to use the Ferranti company archive should contact the archive team at MOSI:

Archives, MOSI, Liverpool Road, Manchester M3 4FP

email: archive@mosi.org.uk

tel: 0161 606 0127 (Tuesday to Saturday)

Contents

"Always Right-Day Or Night"

Introduction

Of all the great British companies, Ferranti would seem to be one that is not often given credit for the quantity and quality of products it produced and the impact it had on the world of electrics and electronics in the commercial and domestic market.
This book gives some history and interesting information about Ferranti and will enable the clock collector to recognise and attribute a identifier and date to their Ferranti Synchronous Electric Clock.
I'm not a professional author but an engineer with a new found keen interest in all things Ferranti, so you will find this book written in a modest style.

Ferranti were of of the main manufacturers of synchronous clocks after Smiths English Clocks in the UK. Smiths had been in the clock and instrument market for some time but entered the synchronous electric clock arena at about the same time as Ferranti or maybe just slightly before. Ferranti synchronous clocks are still available on popular auction sites and car-boot sales but many are lying unused in the shed or roof space of houses.

This book gives the reader some of the history and background to Ferranti's clock manufacturing endeavours, but is not a full and detailed account of everything the company did and the politics behind those decisions. Other publications fulfil that intent and indeed the archives at the Museum of Science and Industry in Manchester has a vast collection of documents and artefacts for the keen investigator.
The records in this book are from the catalogues that have been stored in the Ferranti collection and some from my own collection and so may not include every clock produced as there is not a catalogue for every year. However, with 272 examples, I think that covers the majority.
Ferranti did sell movements without a case so many clock cases by other makers, radios, or other items of furniture, may have a Ferranti movement fitted.

In 1930 the British Clock industry was almost non-existent and the market was covered almost completely by imported clocks. Companies from outside the trade realised they could enter the market with a clock powered by a synchronous motor - a new concept at this time - and capture some of the market.
By 1935 electric clock production was at around 100,000 and in 1937 around 165,000. This was still a small percentage of the market.
After 1940 the government increased the import duty on clocks and set quotas on mechanical clocks.
At the end of 1932 there were at least 8 manufacturers of electric clocks and they formed the Synchronous Clock Conference whose aim it was to make electric clocks more popular.
It is claimed that Smiths made 90% of the clocks in this country; at their height of manufacturing Smiths were making up to 55,000 alarm clocks per week and probably 10 times that in timepieces.
Ferranti aimed to make 1000 alarm clock and just under 3000 timepiece clocks per week.
What is surprising is that Ferranti were not in the top 5 companies on quantity of clocks sold - but they did last until just before electronic clocks captured the market.

"Running cost - Penny a Quarter"

Overview of Ferranti

The history of Ferranti is a large and interesting subject and I do not intend to cover it here, but I have just set the scene for the start of the business to the production of clocks.
In later years the company made a multitude of products especially in the defence and computing areas - delivering the UK's first commercial computer the "Mark 1" in 1951.
I truly believe the work of the Ferranti company has been under-recognised.

Sebastian Ziani de Ferranti was born in Liverpool on April 9th 1864. In his early teens he had starting making electrical machines. He first worked for Siemens in 1881 and then in 1882 formed Ferranti, Thompson and Ince Ltd. An early venture provided electric lighting for a hotel in London, using a steam driven dynamo generator. Over the following years the Ferranti company expanded enormously. Electrical generators, transformers, meters and transmission methods were designed, built and implemented. Having been instrumental in setting the standards for electrical transmission at 10kV and 50Hz AC, and after the 1st World War he again turned his mind to domestic products. After all, electrical domestic appliances would create demand for electrical power supply.

In the late 1920s and early 1930s the Domestic Appliances Department, at Hollinwood, Manchester, resumed making electric fires, water heaters, Gramophones, radios and their components and a range of other products including, in 1931/1932 Clocks.
In 1930 Sir Vincent de Ferranti became chairman of Ferranti Ltd and it is he who took the company into clock production.

Hollinwood Factory 1935

Original held at MOSI (ref 1996.10/10/5/11)

The Domestic Appliance Department

The Domestic Appliance Department was set up originally in 1912 principally to manufacture electric fires, cookers, grills and irons. The department was closed down during the first world war and the cooker and grill interests were sold to Jackson Electric Stove Co.
In 1926 the Domestic Appliance Department was once again formed to manufacture electric fires and domestic water heaters based at Hollinwood. In late 1931/ early 1932 the department began to manufacture clocks. The department moved to the Moston factory in 1937, where radios and television sets were also produced.
They manufactured clocks until March 1957 when it stopped and the department was closed down with some sections being sold off.

In 1935 Ferranti was was invited to display some of it's clocks at the Royal Academy Exhibition of British Art in Industry. Two W.N.Duffy designed clocks were on show.

Clocks on the testing rack at Hollinwood 1935

Original held at MOSI (ref 1996.10/10/5/11)

The Ferranti factory at Hollinwood around 1932.
On the rack, you can see Model Numbers 1,2 and 3 in various finishes of bakelite case.

Original held at MOSI (ref 1996.10/3/3/10107)

The Early Years and the drive to make Clocks

During the late 1920s and into the early 1930s the improvement in supply of controlled AC mains had led to the development of the synchronous electric motor driven clock. Up until this point it was more often a mechanical movement with electric (battery) powered winding. Designers had caught on to the fact that an electric synchronous motor driven clock would not need an escapement for controlling the rate of the clock as this would be controlled by the delivery of the controlled AC mains supply. It also meant no spring was required. Clock movements could now be made more cheaply as two expensive components were no longer required.
In 1918 Henry Warren had developed and patented his synchronous motor. The Warren and Telechron story is a book in itself, suffice to say that by 1929 Warren had convinced power generating companies to introduce Master Clocks into the grid and so controlling the AC frequency, put in place some excellent marketing, and had produced some fabulous clocks such as the Telechron Model 700 'Electroalarm'. The US public were warming to electric synchronous clocks and sales were growing.

On 22nd December 1930 a memo entitled 'NEW DEVELOPMENTS - ELECTRIC CLOCKS' from Ashton Cooper GM of Ferranti Canada stated that sales of the synchronous motor type clock had gone up "leaps and bounds". He also noted that General Electric's distribution of these clocks had moved from electrical dealers to Jewellers and that was perhaps a better sales channel.
He goes on to ask Vincent de Ferranti if he had given the subject any thought and, if he had, could Ferranti manufacture a clock for the North American market.

The reply sent 31st December was short but decisive "VERY INTERESTED TO RECEIVE YOUR LETTER NO 3488 ON ELECTRIC CLOCKS WAS DISCUSSING VERY POINTS YOU RAISED THIS MORNING AND PROPOSE TO MANUFACTURE PLEASE SEND ALL INFORMATION THAT YOU THINK RELEVANT..."

By 1931 the Warren Master clocks were also controlling the UK power stations, under the Synclock name; and Synclock introduced the first synchronous motor powered clock to the UK. In June 1931 British Sangamo were also manufacturing synchronous electric motor clocks.

In January 1931 it would appear that Ferranti were in possession of various electric clocks for examination from makers like General Electric and Sangamo. The engineers at Ferranti surmised that the many and comprehensive Warren patents had not been infringed because the Sangamo and GE clocks were hand starting. The Ferranti engineers were also looking at metering devices which also had synchronous motors.

In March 1931 correspondence shows that Ferranti were in talks with a clock manufacturer in Czechoslovakia about their movement and whether Ferranti could buy the patent rights and produce the movement in the UK. The key people involved were Wilfred Holmes, Manager of the Instrument Department and R Jelinek. They were in discussions with Mr Selig and Mr Michl.

Discussions were ongoing from February 1931 right through to September 1931.

Royalty payments are discussed with payments up front and a royalty amount paid per clock produced. R Jelinek writes many memos to Vincent de Ferranti putting pressure on for a decision. The records include an unsigned agreement, so I do not know if the agreement was ever made.

Checking through Patent records Robert Michl, from Czechoslovakia, filed two patents in 1922 and these were for a synchronous motor with a non-magnetic rotor running in an AC field.

FIG.3.

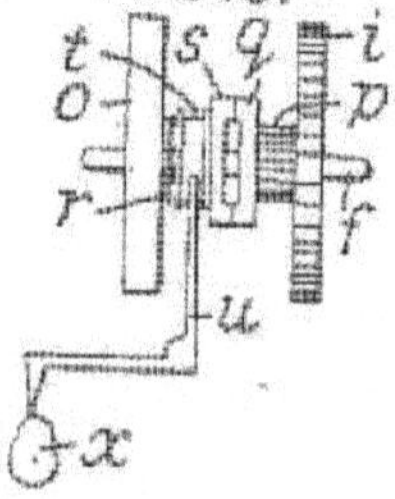

Wilfred Holmes patented two inventions in May 1931. These were the magnetisable rotor running in a bipolar AC field style of motor (GB379383) and the flywheel coupled to the rotor so that when slowing down the rotor has just enough time to synchronise with the AC field (GB384681).

FIG.2.

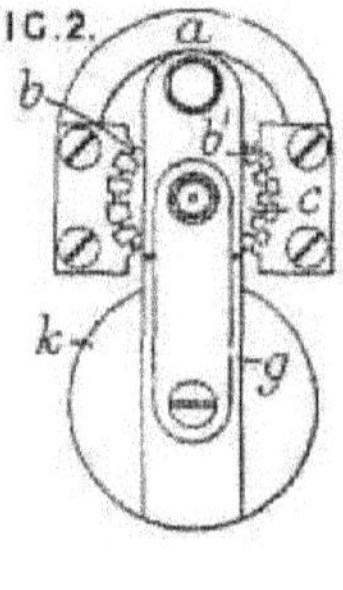

There are significant similarities between the Michl patents and the Ferranti patents.

On 31st August 1931 Holmes filed his Patent application 24461 - detailed in the next section. This shows a complete working clock with a multitude of inventions; a comprehensive set of inventions.

Around June 1931 British Sangamo were in the UK, and an internal memo to Holmes explained that Sangamo were using Bakelite for their clock cases because the cost was around 2/- per case compared to 12/- for a wooden one. In these early days Smiths were using traditional clock case makers/cabinet makers for their quality wooden cases and I suspect Ferranti would have done the same rather than employ skilled cabinet makers. Bakelite cases could be produced on a massive scale once the mould was made - it was also a fascinating new-ish material that traditionally wasn't used for clock cases. Sure enough when Ferranti launched the first four clocks they were all in bakelite cases. Ferranti pressed their own bakelite clock cases and most likely radio cases in the same department.

G.C. ROYCE, PRESIDENT — F.W. ROWNTREE, SECRETARY — A.B. COOPER, GENERAL MANAGER

FERRANTI ELECTRIC LIMITED

METERS - TRANSFORMERS - INSTRUMENTS

FERRANTI

SALES OFFICES
26 NOBLE ST. TORONTO
1070 BLEURY ST. MONTREAL
120 LOMBARD ST. WINNIPEG
510 HASTINGS ST. VANCOUVER

HEAD OFFICE AND FACTORY
TORONTO, ONT.

TELEGRAPH & CABLE ADDRESS
FERRANTI, TORONTO
CODE
WESTERN UNION FIVE LETTER
BENTLEY'S
TELEPHONE LAKESIDE 8800

Ferranti Canada letterhead

The Other Side of the Atlantic

Meanwhile in Canada, Ashton Cooper had been testing a 25Hz motor in his home. His memo to Vincent said that he noted the movement reversed direction with the drop in power when he started his washing machine and the clock ran backwards.

In a September 1931 memo to Vincent, Ashton Cooper details a self-starting synchronous movement that has been demonstrated to him.
The reply from Vincent in the same month is that Ferranti now have a hand starting 50Hz clock motor and can go into production at the end of September. It uses a pure AC field system and dispenses with permanent magnets making economies in production. The 50Hz motor will run at 142.8rpm. [note* actually runs at 166⅔ RPM - maybe a design change]

16 March 1932 a memo from Holmes to Cooper, Holmes states Ferranti UK will supply 1000 25Hz clocks and 1000 60Hz clocks of Models 1,2,3 and 4.
He states the 60Hz version requires a change of two wheels whereas the 25Hz version will need re-tooling. He says that the 50Hz motor runs at 166⅔ RPM and the 60Hz motor runs at 200RPM.
The same month Ferranti claim they will turn out 1000 clocks per day. Quite some claim.

The 1934 catalogue explains that the Ferranti electric clock comes with a centre seconds hand as well as the hour and minute hand. This is a great addition to an electric clock as it is instantly possible to tell if it has stopped. Many companies making electric clocks had been weighing up the pros and cons of self-starting versus non self-starting. Actually, Ferranti always referred to the clocks as 'hand starting'.
The cost of producing a hand starting synchronous motor was a lot cheaper than producing a self-starting motor. And, in many peoples opinion it is better to know that your clock has stopped because the mains went off rather than to not realise because it has restarted and is running but could be hours behind.

Complaints

In the 1930's the national grid was still in its infancy and buying and running a synchronous clock was probably a desire for the latest gadget rather than the the desire for an extremely accurate clock. Power supplies were often interrupted.
On 16 March 1932 The West Gloucester Power Company wrote to Vincent de Ferranti complaining that they will get customer complaints when they cut off the power. He asks if Ferranti can make a clock that will function for a short time with no power.
The reply from Ferranti was "that electric clocks were good for accuracy and in due course we will make a clock that will survive a power break".
The Manager from West Gloucester Power Company replied happily that his clocks will be a good deal more accurate than they have been with him winding them !
Ferranti never did make an electric clock that would survive a power cut and in any case it isn't long before the electricity supply becomes very much more reliable.

Costs

In a memo on to Vincent de Ferranti on 10th December 1931, it was advised that the estimated costs of one of the early clocks in moulded bakelite to be; Material 2 shillings 10d, labour 1 shilling 7d making a total of 4s-6d. this is quoted with 'bought out' dial, cable, springs and glass. Everything else is manufactured at Ferranti. A packing charge is made and packing is 1.8d per clock.

Advert from 1939

Ferranti letterhead late 1920s

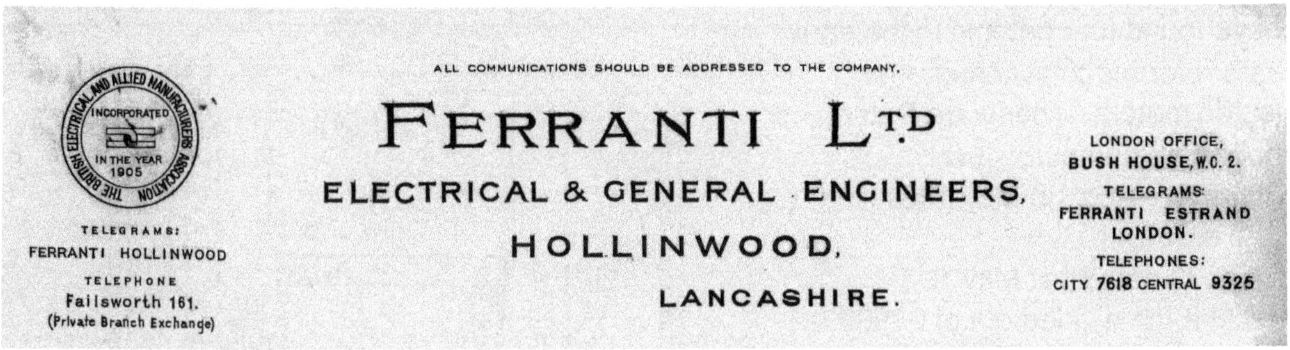
ALL COMMUNICATIONS SHOULD BE ADDRESSED TO THE COMPANY.

FERRANTI LTD

ELECTRICAL & GENERAL ENGINEERS,

HOLLINWOOD,

LANCASHIRE.

THE BRITISH ELECTRICAL AND ALLIED MANUFACTURERS' ASSOCIATION INCORPORATED IN THE YEAR 1905

TELEGRAMS: FERRANTI HOLLINWOOD

TELEPHONE Failsworth 161. (Private Branch Exchange)

LONDON OFFICE, BUSH HOUSE, W.C. 2.

TELEGRAMS: FERRANTI ESTRAND LONDON.

TELEPHONES: CITY 7618 CENTRAL 9325

Trademark Name

The Ferranti dial logo was consistent in style for all the years that clocks were manufactured.

The Ferranti logo used on the early silver dial clocks

This is the logo used on the later clocks with plastic dials.

The Ferranti logo moulded onto a bakelite movement cover from 1933

The Ferranti logo transfer printed onto the back of a clock from 1947.

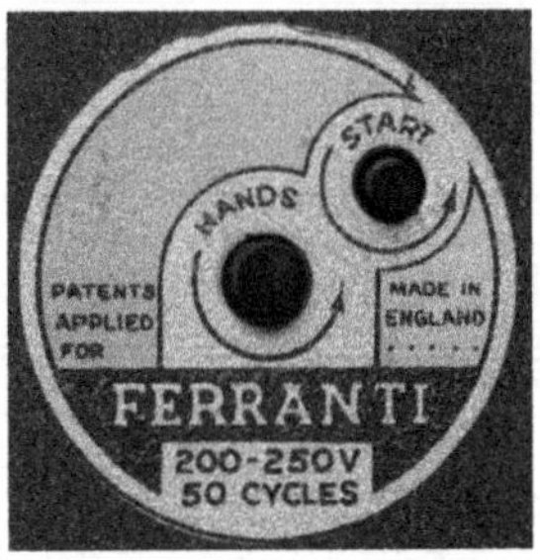

The Ferranti Patents

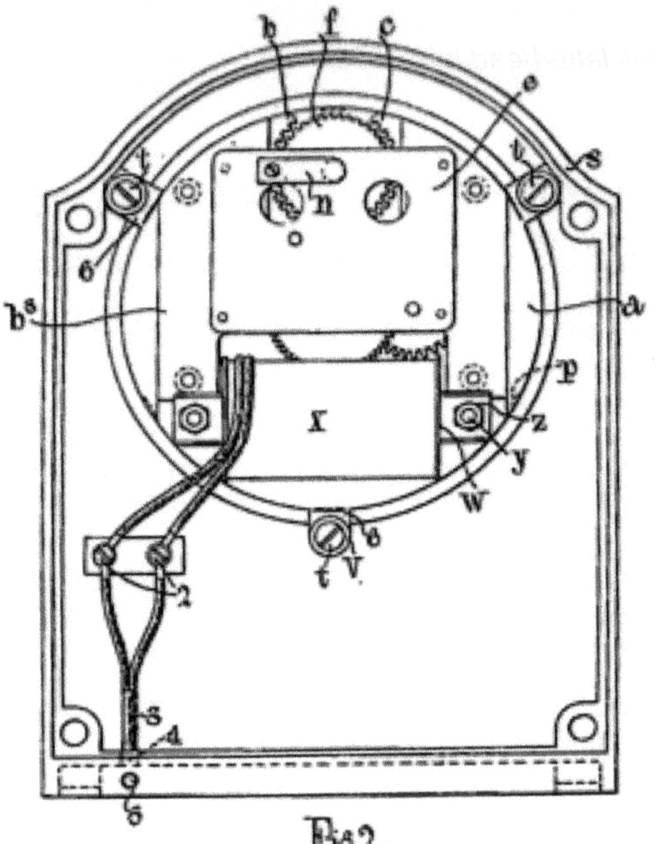

Fig.2.

I have found four patents in the early years referring to synchronous electric motors. These are Patent application numbers:-

12942/31 dated 1st May 1931 (GB379383)

22880/32 dated 1st May 1931 (GB384681, divided out of 379383)

24461/31 dated 31st August 1931 (GB391814)

21801/31 dated 30th July 1931 (GB388739)

The Patent Application numbers that are generally found on the back of Ferranti clock movement cases and are the most relevant are 12942 and 24461.

12942 covers the invention of a synchronous motor comprising a bi-polar constant field system. This patent is demonstrated on a test model. This type of motor was used in every Ferranti clock.

22880 refers to a flywheel being attached either permanently or having some form of decoupling. All the Ferranti motors have flywheels on the rotor spindle. This patent is demonstrated on a test model.

This patent 24461 is shown in a clock model No.1 case and the movement is of the shape of the movement that went into production. It actually covers multiple inventions/ designs, those being:-

1. Self aligning bearings embodying lubricant recesses (for the main rotor spindle)
2. A vibration absorbing mounting
3. Steel front and back plates with brass inserts for wheel spindles to run in
4. Pole pieces and bodies formed as part of the front or back plate
5. A detachable electromagnetic core
6. Core stampings formed of laminated sheet
7. A connecting cable passing through two holes at right angles in the clock casing so as to prevent a direct pull on the cable terminals.

The last patent, 21801 refers to a self starting synchronous electric motor that uses two rotors on the same spindle and will start running in the same direction each time. This principle is similar to many US clocks whereas Ferranti's main rival in this country, Smith's, had self starting motors that could start either way but had a mechanism to reverse the direction of the rotor if needed.
I don't think Ferranti ever used the self starting motor in a domestic clock.

From late 1933 and into 1934 the actual Patent Numbers 391814 and 379383 are put on the back of the clock movement covers.
Patents can take a while to get approved. The main one GB391814 was approved 1st May 1933 and so, allowing for tooling time and using up existing cases, it's most likely the Patent Numbers were introduced late 1933.

Clocks with the new movement are marked as Patents Applied For - even up to 1955. Interestingly, I could find no Patent Applications related to the new movement when production started. And, the new movement has exactly the same design features as the early version except for the introduction of worm wheels.

Other Patents related to synchronous motors approved through the years are:

GB427755 - 30th April 1935 Maurice Kenyon Taylor
GB436145 - 7th october 1935 - Wilfred Holmes
GB477835 - 3rd January 1938 - Eric Grundy
GB484219 - 3rd May 1938 - Henry W Barnes
GB558021 - 15th December 1943 - Sydney W Holmes
GB558022 - 15th December 1943 - Sydney W Holmes
GB662952 - 12th December 1951 - Ernest S Cluderay

Smiths Infringement.

In March 1945 Smiths English Clocks wrote to Ferranti explaining that they may have infringed on a Ferranti patent with the production of a 24hr alarm clock. The infringement was actually that the movement utilised a non-magnetic rotor in an AC magnetic field - a design that Ferranti had been using since 1932. Smiths offer to 'collaborate' on this design but Ferranti politely refuse.
Smiths wanting to copy this type of movement is testament to the excellent quality and design that Ferranti had achieved right from the beginning.

Production and Methods

The Early Movement, 1931 - approx 1945

3½ inches in diameter with mounting lugs built onto the front plate. The mounting lugs hold small rubber mounts to help reduce vibration noise.
The insertion type movement is approx 3¼ inches wide to fit in the bakelite housing

Early movement with front plate removed showing the wheel-work. Front and backplate are brass and are riveted onto larger steel plates used for the rotor magnetic field and for mounting the movement.

As far as I can tell, this is the movement from the war years 1939-1946. The plates are shaped brass and both front and back are the same. Every other part is identical to the early movement with square brass plates.
I have found these movements only in model No's 3, 5 & 9 - which were produced through 1939-1946

Early movement mounted in a model No. 4 clock.
Square brass plates in the middle with iron surrounding to carry the magnetic field.

Wonderful to find the original date stamp, in magenta ink, still visible - 16 June 1933

The regular style of the early models with 3½ dials

An early silvered dial with long thin hands and the longer seconds hand with longer counter balance.
Note also the different five minute markers

The Later movement - approx 1945 and later

The 1947 catalogue proudly announces the newly designed movement both for the timepieces and the alarm models. It goes on to say the new movements retain all the features which have placed Ferranti at the forefront of movement design. These new movements were exceptionally well made and would have been extremely reliable as indeed the previous model was.

The movement had been given some very serious thought. There are no crossed out wheels and it includes two worm-wheels which reduce the wheels required in the train to get the reduction in gearing to drive the hands. The wheels are pressed out and extruded rod is to be used for pinions - so no gear cutting would be required.

The movement itself is considerably smaller. The coil is half the size of the first one - a significant saving to Ferranti as this was an expensive bought in item. Another saving is made by not providing wheel-work for a seconds hand.

Air driven coil winding machines would also be introduced.

This movement is 2¼ inches in diameter. Front and back plate are both brass with riveted on steel formers for the rotor magnetic field.

A comparison of the size reduction of the new movement.

Front view of movements

Rear of the new and
old movements.

Wall Clocks

This is the standard early movement adapted to work in a wall clock. A quick and efficient way to adapt it to enable external hand setting and starting.
The hand setting and starting knob is extended out of the side of the clock case.
When released a pawl on the spring loaded setting bar engages with the first wheel and spins it in the counter clock wise direction to start the motor.
On some later clocks the setting knob is at the 6 o'clock position on the case.

Striking and Chiming Clocks

After some investigation it would appear that Ferranti used a Smith's electric movement for their striking clocks. The rear of the movement is ink stamped with Ferranti but the two Patent numbers belong to Smiths and identify the type of motor and the striking mechanism. I have seen 3 Ferranti chiming clocks with the Patent numbers 366710 and 387108 stamped on the plates. These are Patents that were bought by Smiths in the early 1930s.
It also becomes obvious when the Ferranti and the Smiths chiming clocks are put side by side - the movement is identical.

Smith's Bijou based Clocks

A few examples of Ferranti clocks with Smith's Bijou movements have been found. All the examples with Bijou movements are clocks that were catalogued around the war years. The Bijou movement was in use by Smiths from around 1938. My suspicion is that while Ferranti were dedicating much material and labour to the war effort they were short of movements so bought in the Smiths Bijou to fit and retro-fit some of their clocks. It is also probable that due to the massive backlog of orders in 1945 that they bought in Smiths movements to get the orders fulfilled. The bijou Bakelite cover seen, is stamped Ferranti indicating this was a thought out operation and not just a one off.

No mistake with this Model No. 8 - made to fit a Smiths Bijou pre-1946 movement.
The No.8 was made between 1936 and 1947.

Early Bakelite Moulded Cases

The early bakelite moulded cases that Ferranti made were of a very high quality. The case was accurately pressed including the strengthened holes for the cable. Each screw hole had a metal threaded insert.
Ferranti bakelite cases were formed in-house by 70 ton presses.

Some of the cases have 'Ferranti' stamped underneath.

Early Movement Bakelite Covers

Usually found on a mantel clock. Also the cover for a movement sold on it's own.
Many of the early wooden clocks had a polished 3½ inch metal cover and holder secured to the back of the clock case.

The bakelite cover from a flush fitting clock.
The same cover is used for wall clocks with a hole cut into the side for the setting arm and the rear 'Start and Hands' holes there but not cut out.

Cover and Fixing from the Later Clocks

The rear of a dial (left) from a later movement mantel clock. The movement has a centre nut fixing method and the whole lot is held in place by long screws going right through the clock body and securing into the rear cover.

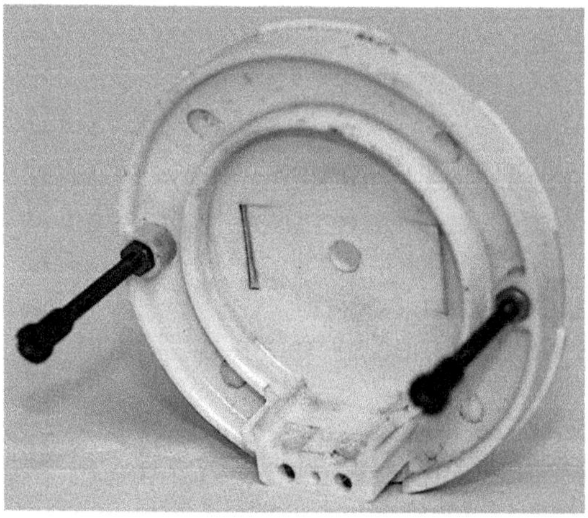

Alarm Clocks

The early Alarm Clock movement.

The Ferranti movement has space to mount the alarm mechanism at the side of the wheel work and has mechanism added to the original wheel layout to produce the alarm functionality. The movement is run on its side in the clock.
The alarm sound is a buzz from the 50Hz attracting a metal strip of steel against the coil armature. Easy and effective.

The buzzer-alarm is described as being "persistent without being strident" !
The alarm mechanism activates every 24hours at the set time and is cancelled with the button on the top of the clock. The alarm-buzzer can be turned of completely by pushing down and turning the button.

The later Alarm Clock movement.

As with the early alarm clock, it is most likely that Ferranti designed the movement from the outset to have the alarm capability. The alarm mechanism integrates with the timepiece very effectively.
The setting button on the rear of the clock shows the time at which the alarm is set.

Guarantee

In an advert from around 1939 Ferranti state that all their clocks are tested at ten times their normal working voltage. They state "They are built to last a lifetime and are subject to our standard 12 month guarantee"

Running Cost

In another advert they state that the clocks' running costs are 1d per quarter to run with electricity at ½d per unit.

Alarm Clock Instructions

The New 'Floodlit Dial Alarm Clock' introduced around 1936

Alarm Clock instructions from 1942

List No. C6a.

FERRANTI

Electric Alarm Clock

MODELS Nos. 7 and 9.

INSTRUCTIONS.

SUITABLE SUPPLIES :

The standard FERRANTI Electric Alarm Clock is suitable for use only on alternating current (A.C.) 50 cycle supplies, 200/250 volts, having time-controlled frequency.

STARTING THE CLOCK :

After connecting the Clock to the mains and setting the hands at the correct time, a twist of the small starting spindle—which will be found at the back of the Clock—will set the Clock running without further attention. It will not need winding or regulating.

SETTING THE ALARM :

The alarm dial will be seen on the lower portion of the main dial, and round half of it is a black mark. The figures against the black mark relate to the night time, or from six in the evening till six in the morning, whilst the figures on the other half of this dial relate to the daytime.

In setting the alarm pointer, therefore, it should be placed against the figure which corresponds to the time when the alarm is to go off at night or in the daytime, as the case may be. The alarm will go off only once in twenty-four hours, and it is not required to be re-set.

EXAMPLE.—If it is required to set the alarm to go off at, say, seven o'clock in the morning, the alarm pointer should be set against the figure seven on the white part of the alarm dial. If the pointer had been set at seven on the black portion, the alarm would go off at seven in the evening.

IMPORTANT.—The small figures on the alarm dial, as they come nearest to the arrow under the centre arbor, give an indication of the time in addition to the main hands, and it is important that the main hands of the clock be turned round until the figures on the alarm dial are in the correct corresponding position. If the clock is first started at, say, ten o'clock in the morning, in setting the hands to ten o'clock they should be turned round until 10 on the white portion of the alarm dial is near the centre of the main dial.

APRIL 1942

In setting this clock, the hands must not be turned backwards.

To stop the alarm, all that is necessary to do is to depress the small knob at the top of the clock.

If it is desired to prevent the alarm going off at any time, the knob should be depressed and given half a turn, when the alarm will not go off again until the knob is released.

FERRANTI ELECTRIC ALARM CLOCK WITH AUTOMATIC FLOODLIGHTING OF DIAL

(MODEL No. 7).

This model is fitted with a 3½ volt bulb (as used in an ordinary flashlamp) inside the case, below the dial. This bulb is energised from the mains.

THE LIGHT IS AUTOMATICALLY switched on at about 12-0 midnight and off at about 8-0 a.m., giving about 8 hours continuous floodlighting of the dial. A separate switch is provided at the back of the Clock to put the light off and on during the floodlighting period, if required. The light will operate only during the 8 hours between midnight and 8-0 a.m.

To replace the bulb, FIRST DISCONNECT THE CLOCK from the mains. Then remove the two large knobs at the back. The hands setting knob is just pulled off, whilst the alarm setting knob is unscrewed in an anti-clockwise direction. There is no need to take off the small starting knob. The back of the Clock can then be removed by taking out the three small screws round the edge.

The bulb is held in a small bracket which will slide out with a gentle pull, when a new bulb can be screwed into position (note how the bulb is screwed into the bracket with its contact against the contact strip). When replacing, make sure that the switch lever is parallel with the bracket, then slide back until it snaps home. Replace the back, taking care that the switch lever and the rubber bush on the lead are in their respective slots.

Note: It is advisable to buy British lamps of branded make, as they will last longer and give more satisfactory results.

Head Office and Works:	*Office and Depot:*
FERRANTI LTD.,	FERRANTI LTD.,
HOLLINWOOD, LANCASHIRE.	BUSH HOUSE, ALDWYCH, LONDON, W.C.2.
Telephone: Failsworth 2000.	Telephone: Temple Bar 6666.
Telegrams: "Ferranti, Hollinwood."	Telegrams: "Ferranti, Bush, London."

Interconnected by Teleprinter.

Reproduced with the permission of MOSI (ref 1996.10/10/3/2)

Instructions that came with the very popular No. 947

FERRANTI

Automatic Electric Alarm Clock

MODEL No. 947

INSTRUCTIONS.

SUITABLE SUPPLIES.

The Standard FERRANTI ELECTRIC ALARM CLOCK is suitable for use on alternating current (A.C.) 200/250 volts, 50 cycle, supplies having time-controlled frequency.

AUTOMATIC FEATURE OF THE FERRANTI ALARM CLOCK.

The FERRANTI ALARM CLOCK works on a 24 hour basis, and, when set, operates once every 24 hours without resetting. For example, if the alarm is set to go off at 7-0 a.m., it will continue to go off at 7-0 a.m. every day, without any resetting of the mechanism at night.

STARTING THE CLOCK.

After connecting the Clock to the mains, set the hands to the correct time, and make sure that, if the time is morning, "A" for "A.M." shows through the observation hole on the Clock face, or, alternatively, if the time is afternoon or evening, that "P" for "P.M." shows. If, on first turning the hands to the correct time, "A" shows when it should be "P", or vice versa, then turn the hands forward another twelve hours and you will see that the letter in the observation hole will have changed to the required one.

Now gently twist the small starting knob—which will be found at the back—and the Clock will run, and continue to do so, without further attention. It will not need winding or regulating.

The starting knob will be seen to revolve continuously, and from this, you will know that the Clock is operating satisfactorily.

SETTING THE ALARM.

The Alarm dial will be seen on the back of the Clock and is divided into two halves, the right-hand side indicating "A.M." and the left-hand side "P.M.". The Alarm setting knob should be turned round in an **anti-clockwise** direction and set against the time the Alarm is to go off.

> **EXAMPLE:**—If the Alarm is required to go off at 7 o'clock in the morning the alarm pointer should be set against 7-0 a.m.

To stop the Alarm, all that it is necessary to do is to depress the small knob at the top of the Clock. The Alarm will operate next day, without further attention. If it is desired to prevent the Alarm going off at any time, the knob should be depressed and given half a turn, when the Alarm will not go off again until the knob is released. This should always be done when the Alarm is not required to function for any length of time.

FERRANTI LTD.

Head Office:
HOLLINWOOD, LANCASHIRE.

Works:
MOSTON,
MANCHESTER, 10,

London Office:
KERN HOUSE, 36, KINGSWAY,
LONDON, W.C.2.

March, 1947

List C.I./1

Ferranti Fused Plug and Safety Sockets

The Ferranti fused plug is fitted internally with two small easily replaceable cartridge fuses, which blow at 0.5 amp, and two spare fuses are accommodated in the plug base.
It fits and standard B.S.S 5-amp socket

The Standard Two-pin Ferrantil Plug, with two ½ amp fuses and two spares

Projecting type socket with Projecting Pin

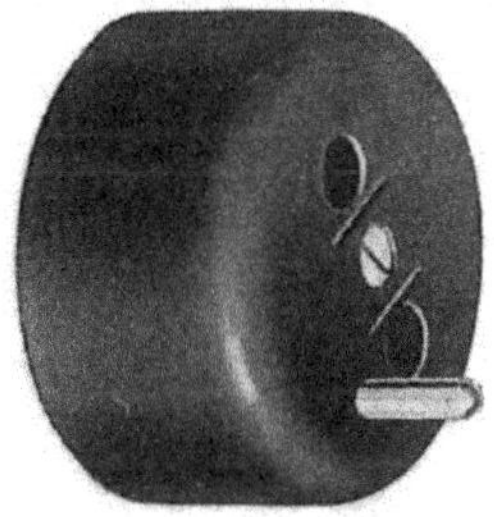

Flush mountlng Socket wlth Projectlng Pin

Illustration of Clock Plug and socket connected to Power Socket. The Ferranti Safety Socket can be supplied either Projecting or Flush type

A projecting pin on the Safety Socket allows only a Ferranti fused plug being used, whence the connection is always safe. The plug is prevented from being inadvertently removed by tightening the screw on the side.

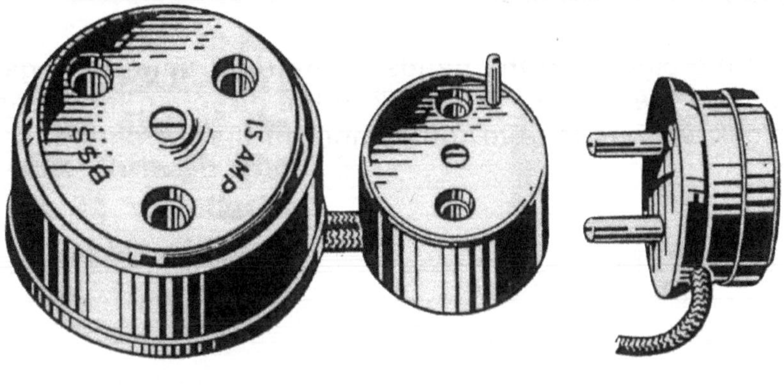

Ferranti Time - Correct time..

Below is the Installation note that is provided with the late 1932 catalogue.

Installation and wiring - The Ferranti clock is far safer, from an electrical point of view , than any other piece of electrical apparatus used in the home, and may be run from an ordinary lamp or power socket provided that the socket is not switched off at any time. A most useful and economical arrangement is as follows.

A standard 5 amp. socket should be permanently wired or looped in parallel to the back of an existing power socket or other outlet in the room.
A few inches of heavy lighting cable are required to connect the small socket in parallel with the live side of the power socket, when the former may be used exclusively for the clock. The flat double vulcanised rubber insulated flexible cable provided with the clock should be cut to the required length and connected to the fused plug.

If the power plug is fitted on a good hard board it only requires a few minutes' work to screw a small socket by its side, but when it is fitted to a plaster wall the size of the pattras or wooden mounting block may have to be increased.

If it is desired to fit a small socket a short distance from the power plug it will be necessary to plug the wall and fit a new small pattras for the clock socket. It should be noted that the wire from the power socket to the clock socket should not be less than 3/.036". The socket and plug are thus protected by the fuse in the main fuse box. The flexible cord and the clock are protected by the half amp double pole fuse in the clock plug.

The cost of various portions of the work should be:
FERRANTI Double Pole Fused Plug and Safety Socket, 2/10 ; 1 ft of insulated cable, 1d ; to this add a few shillings for Wireman's time.

When houses are specially wired for clocks a standard 5 amp socket should be fitted in each room, and they should all be connected in parallel to one pair of 3 amp fuses in the fuse box.

Having connected the clock, set the hands to the right time, then gently twirl the starting spindle at the back of the clock in the direction indicated by the arrow, and the clock will continue to run without further attention.

Design and Marketing

Having examined numerous early Ferranti clocks it is apparent that they were stamped, on the steel surround, in ink with the date of production. Once the movement has been chemically cleaned, which is an industry standard practice, this stamp will no doubt disappear.

From the beginning in 1931 W N Duffy was responsible for clock case design - all his designs numbered and planned out on A1 drawing paper. He was one of the domestic appliances team.

His influences were from general design a the time and the fashionable move towards glass and chrome in the late 1930s. Other manufacturers gave their clocks names to suit the style but Ferranti stuck with 'model number...'. Telechron in America also numbered their clocks although some also had a name. Numbering was far more straightforward and easy to manage from Ferranti's point of view but from a customer point of view I'm sure a name is more endearing.

It is quite likely that where a large retailer stocks Ferranti clocks that they give the clocks a different numbering scheme. I have such an advert - but at this moment I'm not able to determine from whom the advert comes.

Production of their first clocks started in the last quarter of 1931. By November 1931 Ferranti were already talking to other clock manufacturers about fixing the minimum price for their cheapest clocks.

The first four clocks, Model No.1, No. 2, No.3 and No.4, would be in bakelite cases with 3½ inch silver dials with the same hands on all clocks. In the 1932 Catalogue the bakelite finish offered was described as Walnut, Mahogany, Black, Mottled Red, Blue Enamel and Green Enamel.

The early catalogue described clocks available for 200/250 V at 50 cycles and 100/130V at 40,50 or 60 Cycles.

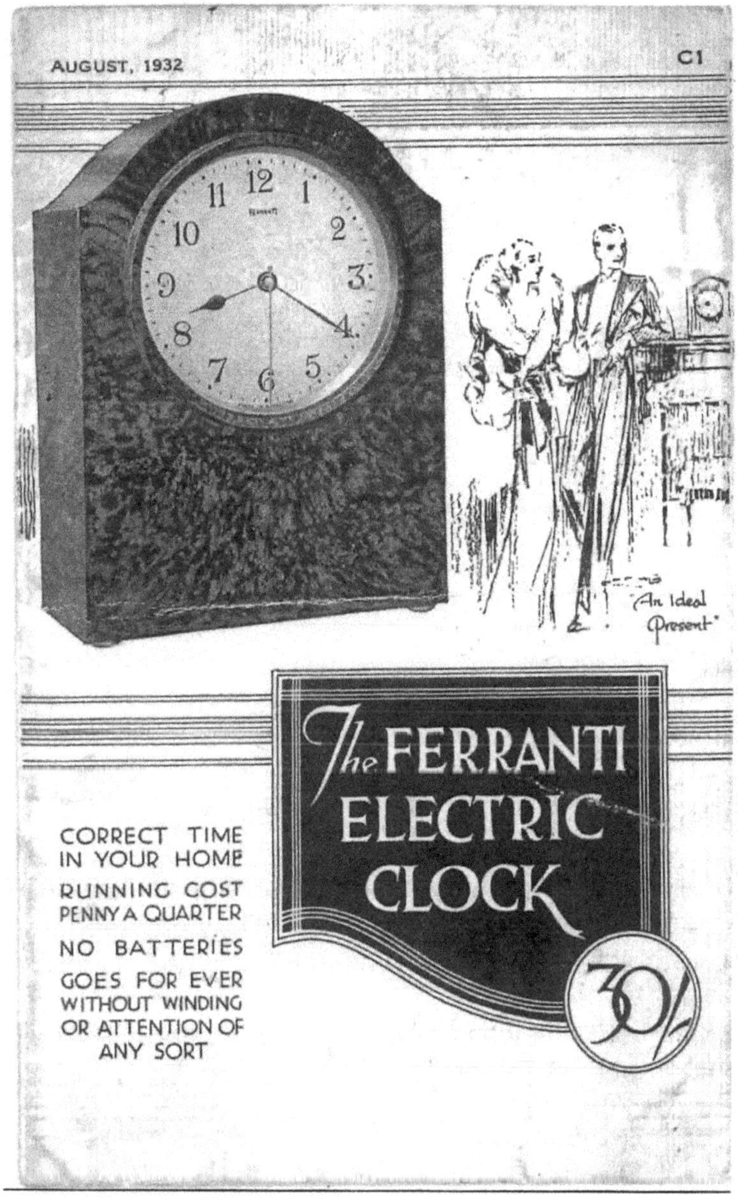

Original held at MOSI (ref 1996.10/10/8/1/20)

Ferranti Offices and Factories related to Clock Manufacture

Head Office and Works - Crown Works Factory, Hollinwood, Lancashire
Factory - Gem Mill, Moston, Manchester

Office and Depot - Connaught House, Great Queen Street, London
Office and Depot - Bush House, Aldwych, London WC2

Office - Kern House, Kingsway, London 1947

Offices abroad

Ferranti Electric Ltd. Mount Dennis, Toronto 9, Ontario, Canada

Ferranti inc.130 West 42nd Street, New York, USA

Distributors

In 1932, as production was gearing up, Ferranti was working out its marketing strategy. They agreed on the following retail outlets for their clocks:-

Pringles, London
Elliotts, London
Russells, London & Liverpool
Makin, Manchester
Hirst Bros, Oldham
Scott, Birmingham
Hector, Glasgow
McRosson, Glasgow
Dimier Bros, London

In return these retailers would only stock Ferranti and Smiths Clocks.

The sole distributor in Ireland for Ferranti clocks was Kelly and Shiel Ltd at the United Works Distillery Road Dublin NE2. They are seen in adverts from the 1940s and 1950s. By 1954 they had showrooms at Fleet Street, Dublin and Drawbridge street Cork.

In March 1932 it was agreed that International Radio and Electric Corporation (a subsidiary of International Telegraph and Telephone Corporation) would become the overseas distributors first starting with sales in Norway, Yugoslavia, Belgium and Spain. The deal was 20-30% off list price.

Wartime Production

During the years affected by the Second World War (1939-1945) Ferranti like many other businesses in the UK were putting all their effort into manufacturing for munitions. Ferranti's factories were turned over to making fuses for bombs and parts for aeroplanes.
Clock production came second.
In 1943 a Ferranti adverts lists just 4 models as part of a 'reduced range to meet wartime conditions'.
These were Model Nos. 3, 5,9 and 27. With prices between 41s 3d and 45s and Purchase Tax from 7s 2d and 10s 4d, I don't suppose Ferranti sold many clocks during these years. They did however take orders for clocks to be supplied when the war years were over.

A departmental memorandum at the end of 1945 from Mr Grundy gives a statement on clock production which would seem to be considering the department's future.
The points in brief are: He is compressing tooling and development costs into the current financial year - allowing a clean start for the next financial year. This would imply the new movement is ready for production. In respect of the original selling price of Ferranti clocks, Grundy states the prices were too low. The reasons being wrong prices and low manufacturing efficiency and high prices of coils and plated parts. Also, in some cases the design itself means labour costs are high.
He says he is happy with the new alarm clock and expects production to start June 1946. The new design and production methods will give maximum reliability. Production changes include producing pinions from extruded rod (no gear cutting) and wheels made from a press tool. Coil winding will be done by Ferranti air driven machines running at 5000 RPM. All together 100 improvements mentioned but not identified.

In July 1945 the Clock department made the following statement:-

Outstanding orders for Utility models 6,000
Outstanding orders for Post war models 100,000

The Program for production was to be: -		
	August	3,000
	September	4,000
	October	5,000
	November	6,000

leading to an ultimate production level of 10,000 per month
This backlog of orders to fulfil would certainly take a while. The clock department was ramping up production and in September 1945 had produced 4281 clocks. That backlog would take some time to clear. The sales team were asked to do their best to fulfil orders from "old friends" and carefully consider new orders of many thousands - quoting a 6 month delivery time if possible.

"Ferranti time - correct time"

1947 Trading

In this year Ferranti plan to manufacture 150,000 timepieces and 50,000 alarm clocks. They expect to make a lower margin on an expensive case than a cheaper one.
Based on his best estimates the cost of producing a timepiece is 19/9 and 19/2 for an alarm clock. (the timepiece price being higher because of fancy case costs). The net selling prices being 23/- and 21/0 for the alarms. Margins of 16% and 8% respectively.
Grundy goes on to say he expects the clock department to operate successfully until 1948 and possible up to 1950.
Interestingly, he discusses overhead costs and the results of reducing them - so he obviously recognised they were very high.

For the production of a timepiece the costs are:-

Materials	6s 7½d
Labour	2s 7½d
Overheads	10s 6d
Total of	19s 9d

for alarm clocks they are:-

Materials	6s 5½d
Labour	2s 6½d
Overheads	10s 2d
Total of	19s 2d

Advert from 1938

The overheads seem to be very high and I suspect these were overheads for the department as a whole. The Department accounts 1948 to 1958 show that 'clocks' made a loss every year except for 1950, with the largest loss of £24 thousand being in 1949.
That sounds a lot but the radio department also made massive losses practically every year except 1953 & 1954.
The radio departments largest loss in 1957 was £841 thousand.!
As a contrast the Fire Control and Instrument department profits were in the region of £400 thousand per department.

This fantastic advert from early June 1932 is the earliest I have been able to find and shows the first four Ferranti clocks to go into production.
All bakelite and all available in the Walnut, Mahogany and mottled colours.

The British Clockmakers Association

In late 1931 four british companies were about to produce larger quantities of the new synchronous electric clocks to capture an inquisitive population. A letter from Everett Edgcumbe to Ferranti asked for some agreement to be made over a minimum price. They stated that they produced their lowest priced clock at 40 shillings and had observed that Smiths then dropped theirs to 35 shillings and now Ferranti dropped theirs to 30 shillings. They needed to stop the vicious process now to maintain any margin of profit.

Late November the minimum price of 30 shillings was agreed between Everett Edgcumbe and Ferranti and would then propose this to Smiths and Sangamo.
Early December Smiths, Ferranti, Sangamo and Everett Edgecumbe all agreed to a minimum price of 30 shillings.

In early 1932 the British Watch and Clock Makers Association was formed with the intention of agreeing prices and lobbying for import duties on foreign imports.
Mr A Gordon Smith was elected as Chairman.
In late 1932 eight companies came together to form the British Synchronous Clock Conference whose aim it was to promote the British Synchronous Electric Clock. These were:- Smiths, British Sangamo, English Clock and Watch Co., Synclock, Temco, Genalex, Synchronomains and Ferranti.

A large clock being proudly displayed before shipping to the customer.

Original held at MOSI (ref 1996.10/10/5/11)

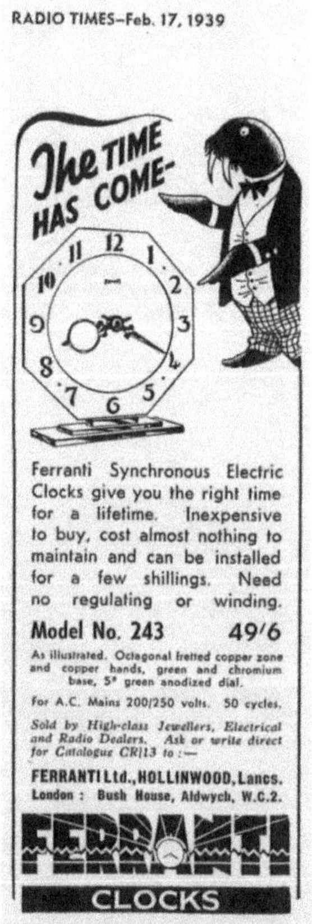

Advert from 1939

Following is a series of humorous adverts from 1945

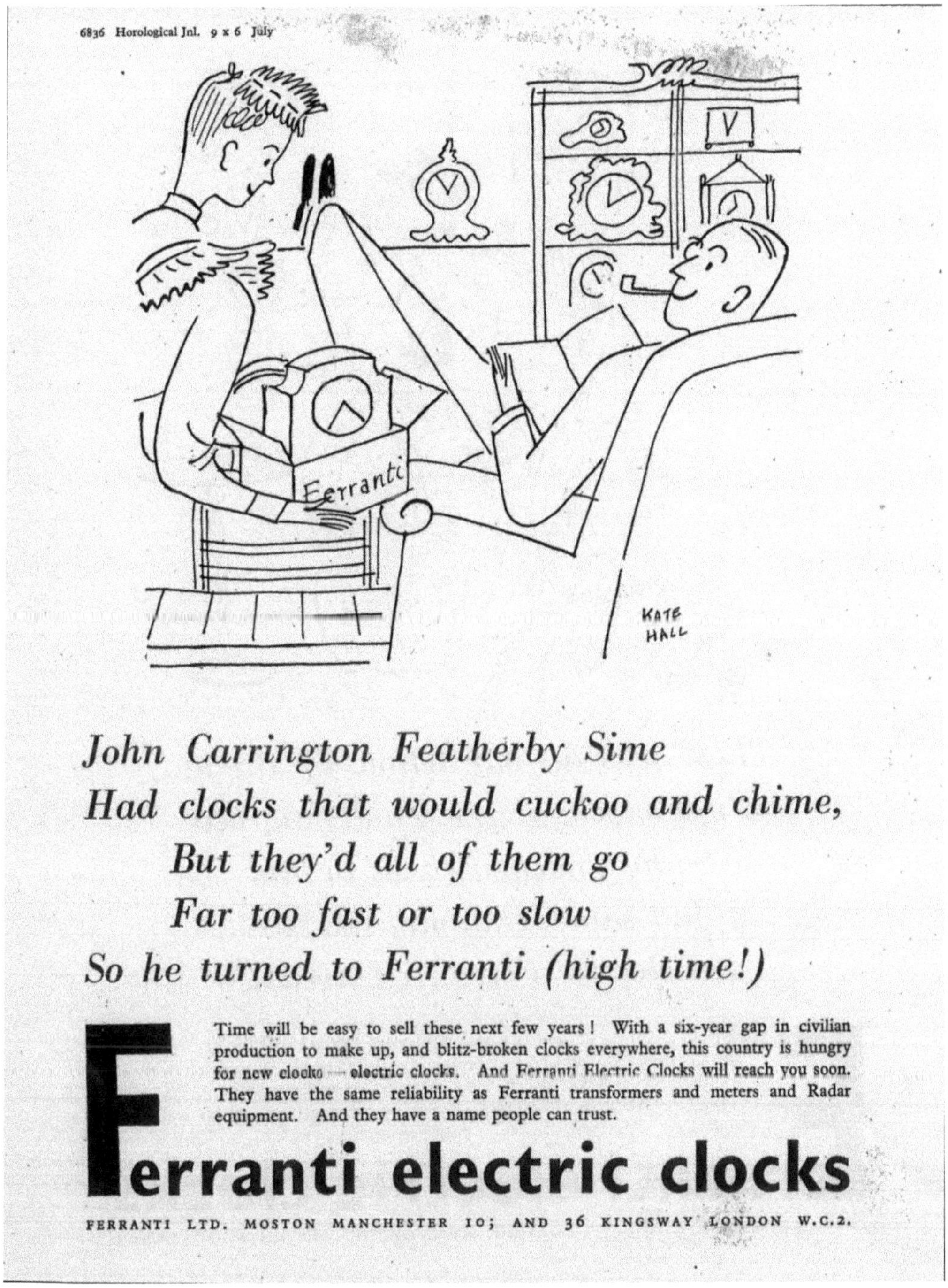

Reproduced with the permission of MOSI (ref 1996.10/3/2/60)

Reproduced with the permission of MOSI

Reproduced with the permission of MOSI

More than meets the eye

THERE'S more than surface good looks to a Ferranti Electric Clock. We believe that it's the works that matter; and we don't see why they shouldn't have some of the limelight (that's why we've shown them here).

Not that we've anything against good looks. The new range of Ferranti Clocks has been designed to make the best use of both modern and traditional materials. It includes clocks in wood cases, in plastics, and clocks which make decorative use of glass and metal. There is a wide range of designs, and of prices. Write to us for further information.

Ferranti

ELECTRIC

CLOCKS

FERRANTI

FERRANTI LTD MOSTON MANCHESTER 10; AND 36 KINGSWAY LONDON WC2

Reproduced with the permission of MOSI

Reproduced with the permission of MOSI

The wonderful Model No. 3   This version from 1938

Available in, Black
Walnut effect Bakelite
Mahogany effect Bakelite
Blue enamel
Green Enamel

No. 3

Earlier versions had a plain silvered dial and were available in Black, Mahogany, Walnut, Mottled Blue, Mottled Green, Mottled Red and Mottled Brown.

This choice applied to Model No.s 1, 2, 3 & 4

Identifying Clocks in the Catalogue.

I should start by saying that there will be clocks with Ferranti movements that are not in this catalogue. I can say that with certainty because I have two. These are very high quality wooden cases made specifically for a customer and fitted with a Ferranti insert movement.
In some cases I have shown pictures of the same clock from more than one year. This is to show the difference in case, dial or hands that may occur over the production period. The differences from early to mid to late (ie dial and hand type) would apply to many models. One example is model no. 3 - which had 2 different case types, 2 dial types and 3 hand types.
The date of the catalogue that from which the picture came is show against each clock.

Notes.

1932

From 1932 to around 1936 3½ dial clocks were nearly all silvered dials with plain hands of the ‘spade’ type. The seconds hand on some of the early Models 1 & 2 reached to the edge of the dial and had a noticeable counter balance. All other models have a short seconds hand with a tiny counter balance.

1936

Striking and Chiming clocks are introduced. At the moment I suspect these were Smiths movements stamped with the Ferranti name.

1937

Somewhere between 1936 and 1938 production moved towards ‘fancy clocks’, those made of glass and chrome etc. Many plain models were dropped and new ones introduced.
At this time the basic models that did continue were furnished with dials consisting of a pinned on silvered chapter ring and cream middle, especially noticeable on the 3½ dial range. The hands also changed to a more open type
The venerable model no. 3, along with No 4 and 5 adopted a chrome bezel.

1939-1945

During the war years production was reduced to meet wartime conditions. The department was tasked with building fuzes and other devices for military use.
Four ‘proven’ models were kept in production; these were Mantel Clock Model No’s 3 and 5, alarm clock No. 9 and Wall Clock No.27.
It is likely that the plain cream metal dial was used during the 1939-1945 war years.
This dial is also very thin and hard to find in good condition. The Smiths Bijou movement was used in some clocks at this time.

1947 and onwards

After the second world war Ferranti restarted clock production with vigour. There was lost time to make up for and back orders for clocks other than the 4 types made during the war year.
The early movement is used with a plain white plastic dial and open hands for many clocks in the 1947 catalogue. I'm sure though, that it would have taken a while to use up stock of the early movement and fully transition to the new one. Especially with wall clocks.

A new movement had been designed and plastics had improved considerably. The budget clocks now incorporated a white plastic dial that also served as the mounting for the movement behind - a very neat and economical solution.
Practically all clocks had open style hands.
Most noticeable will be the lack of a seconds hand - the new movement is not built to provide one.
None of the catalogues mention the insertion movements from this point.
It is possible that the Smiths Bijou movement was used for a few years to catch up with a backlog of orders.

Movements

Ferranti were advertising their No. 30 and No.70 movement from as early as June 1933. The movements, 3.5 inches and 6 inches respectively were sold with a description including "..suitable for replacing unreliable spring driven movements". From 1939 onwards it would appear that Ferranti did not offer movements as a separate item - so when looking at a clock with a Ferranti movement that is not in the catalogue the reader should consider that this could be a case made before 1939 and has a Ferranti movement built into it. Likewise it could be a later case using an early spare insertion movement. The 3.5 inch insertion movement also happens to be the same size that Smith's used.

Sockets, Plug and Leads

From 1947 these are no longer advertised. I would suspect that modern plastics and improvements in wiring standards superseded the Ferranti system. For some reason pre-1946 mantel clocks came with 7 foot of maroon flexible braided wire.
In the 1947 catalogue says that mantel clocks come with a 6 foot lead - probably a small cost saving exercise or maybe to a division of a much larger manufactured length that the cable is cut from.

The Catalogue of clocks is presented in the following order:-

3½ inch Dial Mantel Clocks

1934

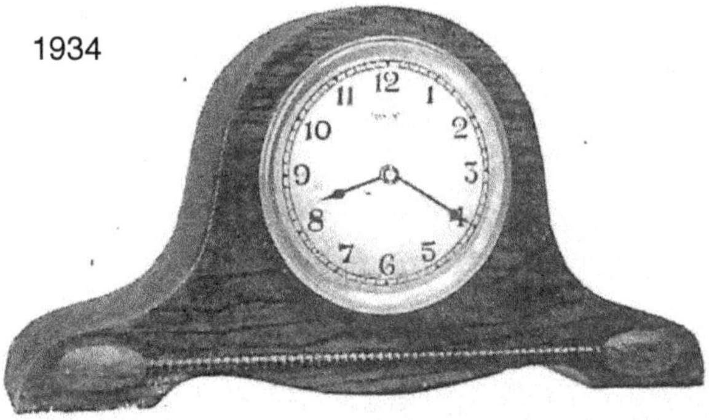

No. 31. **35/–**
Jacobean, Chromium Bezel, 3½″ dial.

1934

No. 32. **37/6**
Polished Oak, Chromium Bezel, 3½″ dial.

1938

No. 33

MODEL No. 33. **Jacobean.** **37/6**

3½ in. Cream Dial with Silvered Zone, and **Chromium Bezel.**

Height, 6 in. Width, 6¾ in. Depth, 3¼ in.

1934

No. 33. **37/6**
Jacobean, Chromium Bezel, 3½″ dial.

1947

No. 33—Walnut, Mahogany, Light Oak.

All images are courtesy of MOSI

3½ inch Dial Mantel Clocks

1934

No. 34. **39/–**
Jacobean, Chromium Bezel, 3½″ dial.

1934

No. 35. **40/–**
Polished Mahogany, Chromium Bezel, 3½″ dial.

No. 35a. Polished Oak. **40/–**

1934

No. 36. **42/–**
Polished Oak, Chromium Bezel, 3½″ dial.

1932

No. 39.
Polished Walnut.
Chromium Bezel,
3½″ dial ... **50/–**

1934

No. 37. **42/–**
Inlaid Walnut, Chromium Bezel, 3½″ dial.

All images are courtesy of MOSI

3½ inch Dial Mantel Clocks

No. 38A

1938

MODEL No. 38A 49/6

Polished Oak.

$3\frac{1}{2}$ in. Cream Dial
with Silvered Zone,
and **Chromium Bezel.**

Height, $6\frac{1}{4}$ in. Width, 9 in.
Depth, $3\frac{1}{4}$ in.

1934

No. 38. **42/-**
Polished Oak, Chromium Bezel, $3\frac{1}{2}''$ dial.

No. 38a. **49/6**
Polished Oak, Chromium Bezel,
$3\frac{1}{2}''$ Square dial.

1934

No. 40. Art Walnut.
Chromium Bezel,
$3\frac{1}{2}''$ dial ... **55/-**

1934

No. 41. **57/6**
Polished Mahogany, Chromium Bezel,
$3\frac{1}{2}''$ dial.

1934

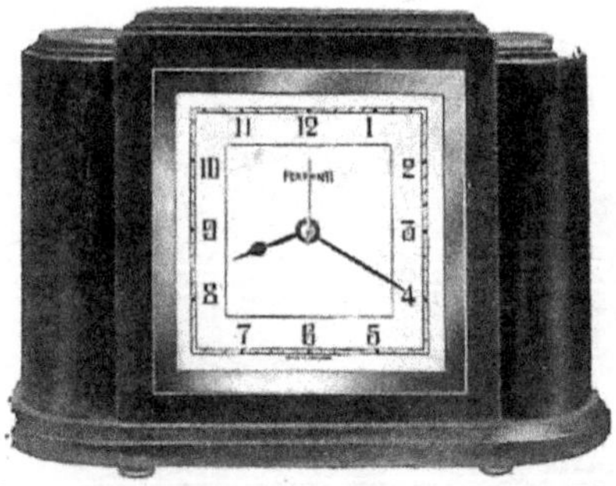

No. 41a. **63/-**
Polished Mahogany, Chromium Bezel,
$3\frac{1}{2}''$ dial.

All images are courtesy of MOSI

3½ inch Dial Mantel Clocks

1934

No. 42.
Inlaid Walnut.
Chromium Bezel,
$3\frac{1}{2}''$ dial ... **57/6**

1934

No. 44. **63/–**
Burr Walnut, Chromium Bezel, $3\frac{1}{2}''$ dial.

1947

No. 45—Dark Oak.

MODEL No. 45. **Walnut.** **60/-**

$3\frac{1}{2}$ in. Cream Dial with Silvered Zone, and **Chromium Bezel.**

Height, $5\frac{1}{2}$ in. Width, $7\frac{1}{4}$ in. Depth, $3\frac{1}{4}$ in.

1938

No. 45

1938

MODEL No. 46. **Oak.** **55/-**

$3\frac{1}{2}$ in. Cream Dial
with Silvered Zone,
and **Chromium Bezel.**

Height, $6\frac{1}{4}$ in. Width, 10 in.
Depth, $3\frac{1}{2}$ in.

No. 46

All images are courtesy of MOSI

3½ inch Dial Mantel Clocks

1938

MODEL No. 47 65/-

Walnut—with **Ebony** Base.

3½ in. Cream Dial with Silvered Zone, and **Chromium Bezel.**

Height, 6¾ in. Width, 7⅞ in. Depth, 3¾ in.

No. 47

1934

No. 51. **35/-**
Jacobean Case, Chromium Bezel, 3½″ dial.

1934

No. 52. **42/-**
Highly polished Sycamore Case with ebonised base, Chromium Bezel, 3½″ dial.

1934

No. 53. **50/-**
Amboyna and Macassar Case, Chromium Bezel, 3½″ dial.

1934

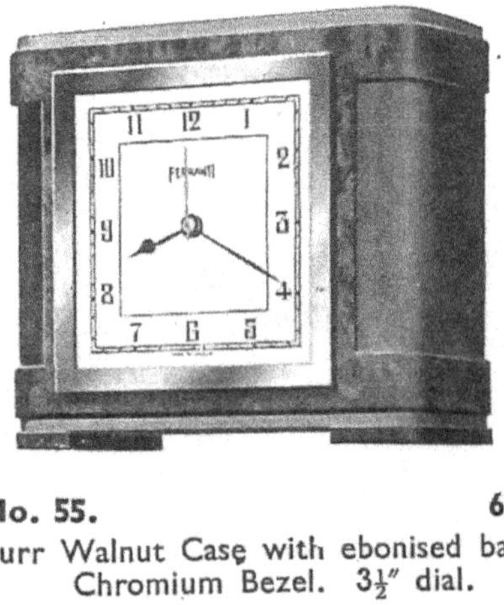

No. 55. **63/-**
Burr Walnut Case with ebonised base, Chromium Bezel. 3½″ dial.

All images are courtesy of MOSI

3½ inch Dial Mantel Clocks

1938

MODEL No. 54. **Walnut.** **57/6**

3½ in. Cream Dial with Silvered Zone, and **Chromium Bezel.**

Height, 5½ in. Width, 8 in. Depth, 3¼ in.

No. 54

1934

No. 54. **57/6**

Walnut Case, Chromium Bezel. 3½" dial.

Nos. 57-8-9

1938

MODEL No. 57. **Oak.** **60/-**

MODEL No. 58. **Walnut.** **63/-**

MODEL No. 59. **Mahogany.** **63/-**

3½ in. Cream Dial with Silvered Zone, and **Chromium Bezel.**

Height, 5¾ in. Width, 8¼ in. Depth 3 in.

All images are courtesy of MOSI

3½ inch Dial Mantel Clocks

1936

No. 130. Jacobean. **37/6**
3½″ Silvered Dial, Chromium Bezel.

No. 130—Dark Oak.

1947

1938

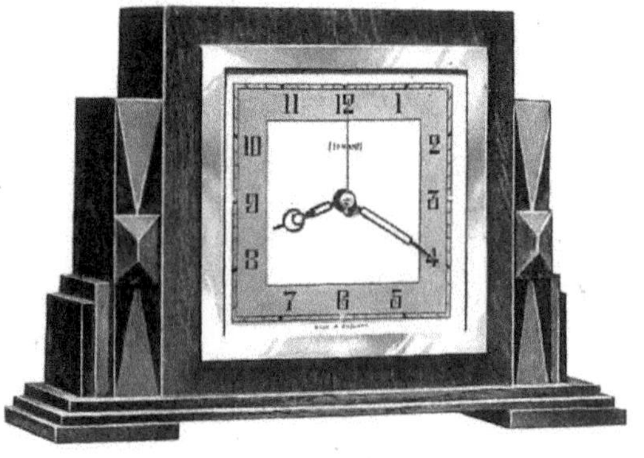

No. 130

MODEL No. 130. **Jacobean.** **37/6**

3½ in. Cream Dial with Silvered Zone, and **Chromium Bezel.**

Height, 5¾ in. Width, 8¼ in. Depth, 3¼ in.

1936

No. 131. Jacobean. **37/6**
3½″ Silvered Dial, Chromium Bezel.

MODEL No. 131. **Jacobean.** **37/6**

3½ in. Cream Dial with Silvered Zone, and **Chromium Bezel.**

Height, 6¼ in. Width, 8¼ in. Depth, 3¼ in.

1938

No. 131

All images are courtesy of MOSI

3½ inch Dial Mantel Clocks

1936

No. 132. Polished Oak. 40/-
3½″ Silvered Dial, Chromium Bezel.

No. 132—Medium Oak.

1947

1938

MODEL No. 132. **Oak.** **40/-**

3½ in. Cream Dial with Silvered Zone, and **Chromium Bezel.**

Height, 5¾ in. Width, 9½ in. Depth, 3¼ in.

1938

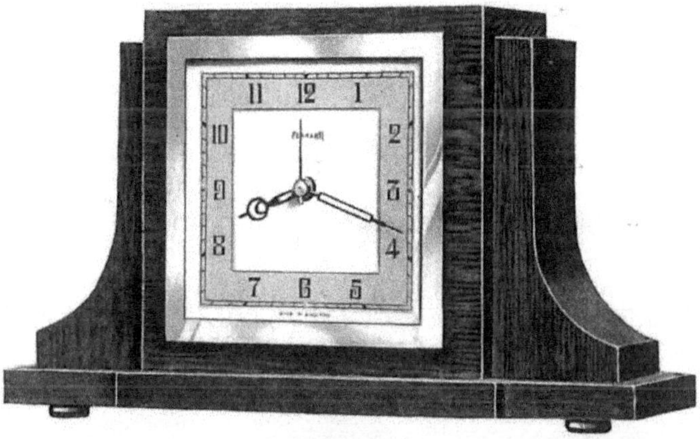

No. 132

All images are courtesy of MOSI

3½ inch Dial Mantel Clocks

MODEL No. 162. **Walnut.** **42/-**

MODEL No. 163. **Oak.** **40/-**

3½ in. Cream Dial with Silvered Zone,
and **Chromium Bezel.**

Height, 6 in. Width, 6¼ in. Depth, 3¼ in.

1938

No. 162-3

No. 160

MODEL No. 160. **Oak.** **32/6**

3½ in. Cream Dial with Silvered Zone,
and **Chromium Bezel.**

Height, 5½ in. Width, 7 in. Depth, 3 in.

No. 161

1938

MODEL No. 161. **Oak.** **35/-**

3½ in. Cream Dial
with Silvered Zone,
and **Chromium Bezel.**

Height, 5½ in. Width, 8 in.
Depth, 3 in.

1947

No. 161—Walnut, Mahogany, Light Oak.

All images are courtesy of MOSI

3½ inch Dial Mantel Clocks

1938

MODEL No. 164. **Walnut.** 50/-

3½ in. Cream Dial with Silvered Zone, and **Chromium Bezel.**

Height, 5¾ in. Width, 8¼ in. Depth, 3 in.

No. 164

1938

MODEL No. 165. **Mahogany.** 50/-

3½ in. Cream Dial with Silvered Zone, and **Chromium Bezel.**

Height, 5½ in. Width, 9¾ in. Depth, 4 in.

No. 165

1938

Model No. 253. Oak. 29/6
Model No. 254. Walnut. 35/-
3½" fret silvered zone and chromium bezel. Silvered hands.
Height 5¼". Width 6¼." Depth 3".

All images are courtesy of MOSI

No. 300—Dark Oak.

1947

No. 301—Dark Oak.

1947

1947 **No. 303**—Dark Oak.

1947

No. 310—Walnut or Australian Silky Oak with Sycamore base.

1947

No. 311—Dark Oak.

All images are courtesy of MOSI

3½ inch Dial Mantel Clocks

No. 330—Medium Oak.

1947

No. 331—Medium Oak.

1947

1947

No. 332—Medium Oak.

1947

No. 336—Walnut with Zebrana facings or Pomele Mahogany with Sycamore facings.

1952

No. 335—Walnut or Pomele Mahogany with Ebonised plinth.

All images are courtesy of MOSI

3½ Inch Dial Clocks c1950 - no catalogue entry, possibly not released

No. 302

No. 304

No. 306

No. 305

No. 307

All images are courtesy of MOSI

3½ inch Dial Clocks c1950 - no catalogue entry, possibly not released

No. 308

No. 314

No. 309

No. 313

All images are courtesy of MOSI

4½ inch Dial Mantel Clocks

Nos. 400, 401, 402, 403 – Dark Oak veneer. Black numerals on Silvered zone. Silver-plated and lacquered hands.

1955

No. 400

1955

No. 401

1955

No. 403

1955

No. 402

All images are courtesy of MOSI

5 inch Dial Mantel Clocks

1936

No. 88. Oak. **70/–**
No. 89. Mahogany. **75/–**
No. 90. Burr Walnut. **90/–**
5″ Silvered Dial,
Chromium Bezel.

MODEL No. 166. **Oak.** 70/-
MODEL No. 167. **Walnut.** 75/-
MODEL No. 168. **Mahogany.** 75/-

5 in. Cream Dial with Silvered Zone,
and **Chromium Bezel.**

Height, 7¼ in. Width, 7¼ in. Depth, 3¾ in.

1938

Nos. 166-7-8

MODEL No. 169. **Oak.** 70/-
MODEL No. 170. **Walnut.** 75/-

5 in. Silvered Zone,
and **Chromium Bezel.**

Height, 7 in. Width, 8¼ in. Depth, 4 in.

1938

Nos. 169-70

1947

No. 170—Medium Oak or Walnut, with Sycamore side pieces. 5″ dial. Silvered zone.

All images are courtesy of MOSI

5 inch Dial Mantel Clocks

MODEL No. 174 **Walnut.** 70/- 1938

6 in. Fret Zone,
and **Chromium Bezel.**

Height, 8¾ in. Width, 11¼ in.
Depth, 3 in.

Model No. 246. 63/-
Walnut case with chromium hair-line bezel and mounting. This clock is specially shallow for a narrow mantelpiece. 5″ dial with fret zone and silver finish.
Height 8¼″. Width 9″. Depth 2¾″.

1938

Nos. 171-2-3

MODEL No. 171. **Oak.** 55/-

MODEL No. 172. **Walnut.** 60/-

MODEL No. 173. **Mahogany.** 60/-

6 in. Cream Dial with
Silvered Zone,
and **Chromium Bezel.**

Height, 8½ in. Width, 10¼ in.
Depth, 3½ in.

1938

Model No. 247. Oak. **53/–**
Model No. 248. Walnut. **56/–**

Open dial with chromium hair-line bezel, hands and feet.
5″ dial with silvered zone.
Height 6½″. Width 7″. Depth 2¾″.

1938

5 inch Dial Mantel Clocks

No. 554

1955

No. 554 – Walnut or Oak veneer with Black edging. Embossed Gilt numerals on Cream zone. Cream hands.

No. 555 – Walnut veneer with Black edging and Green zone. Oak veneer with Black edging and Rich Cream zone. Embossed Gilt numerals. Rich Cream hands.

No. 556 – Walnut veneer with Cream edging and Rich Cream zone. Oak veneer with Cream edging and Green zone. Embossed Gilt numerals. Rich Cream hands.

No. 555

1955

No. 556

1955

All images are courtesy of MOSI

6 inch Dial Mantel Clocks

No. 75. Walnut. **70/–**
No. 76. Mahogany. **70/–**
6″ dials and Chromium Bezels.

1934

No. 77. Jacobean. 55/–
6″ Silvered Dial, Chromium Bezel.

1936

MODEL No. 85. **Oak.** **75/-**

MODEL No. 87. **Walnut.** **95/-**

6 in. Cream Dial with Silvered Zone,
and **Chromium Bezel.**

Height, 8½ in. Width, 7¾ in. Depth, 3¼ in.

1938 Nos. 85-7

No. 88.	Oak.	**70/–**
No. 89.	Mahogany.	**75/–**
No. 90.	Burr Walnut.	**90/–**

6″ Dial.
Chromium Bezel.

1934

All images are courtesy of MOSI

6 inch Dial Mantel Clocks

1936

No. 136. **85/-**
Oak, Ebonised Side Pieces and Plinth and Chromium Straps.

No. 137. **90/-**
Walnut, Dark Walnut Side Pieces and Plinth and Chromium Straps.
6″ × 6″ Silvered Dial,
Chromium Bezel.

1938

Nos. 136-7

MODEL No. 136. **Oak.** **85/-**

MODEL No. 137. **Walnut.** **90/-**

Ebonised Side Pieces, and Plinth with Chromium Straps.

6 in. Cream Dial with Silvered Zone, and **Chromium Bezel.**

Height, 7½ in. Width, 8¼ in. Depth, 3¼ in.

No. 140. Oak. **77/6**
No. 141. Walnut. **90/-**

6″ Dial.
Silvered Fret Zone.
Chromium Bezel.

Height	8″
Width	10″
Depth	3¼″

1936

:h 2¼″.

1938

Model No. 251. Oak. ...**60/-**
Model No. 252. Walnut. **63/-**
This is another shallow depth Clock designed for narrow mantelpieces, having the 6″ dial covered by plate glass and held by a chromium and ebony support. Silvered hands.
Height 8½″. Width 8½″.
Depth 3″.

All images are courtesy of MOSI

6 inch Dial Mantel Clocks

No 316—Dark Oak.
6″ Silvered zone.
1947

No. 317—Dark Oak.
6″ Silvered zone.
1947

No. 320—Dark Oak.
6″ Silvered zone.
1947

All images are courtesy of MOSI

6 x 8 inch Dial Mantel Clocks

No. 63. Oak. **84/–**
No. 64. Mahogany. **90/–**

6″ × 8″ Silvered Dial,
Chromium Bezel.

1936

No. 69. **95/–**
Hungarian Ash and Ebony.
No. 69a. **90/–**
Walnut and Ebony.
Dial 6″ × 8″.
Chromium Bezel.

1934

MODEL No. 177. **Oak.** **84/-**
MODEL No. 178. **Walnut.** **97/6**
MODEL No. 179. **Mahogany.** **92/6**

6 in. × 8 in. Cream Dial with Silvered Zone, and **Chromium Bezel.**

Height, 9¾ in. Width, 9¾ in. Depth, 3½ in.

1938

Nos. 177-8-9

All images are courtesy of MOSI

8 x 6 inch Dial Mantel Clocks

No. 68. Walnut inlaid with Whitewood. **95/-**

1936 8″ × 6″ Silvered Dial,

Chromium Bezel.

No. 138. **92/6**

Solid Walnut, Ebonised Side Pieces and Feet.

8″ × 6″ Silvered Dial,

Chromium Bezel. 1936

1938

MODEL No. 61. **Oak.** **84/-**

MODEL No. 62. **Walnut.** **95/-**

MODEL No. 191. **Mahogany.** **95/-**

8 in. × 6 in. Cream Dial with Silvered Zone, and **Chromium Bezel.**

Height, 8 in. Width, 11 in.
Depth, 3½ in.

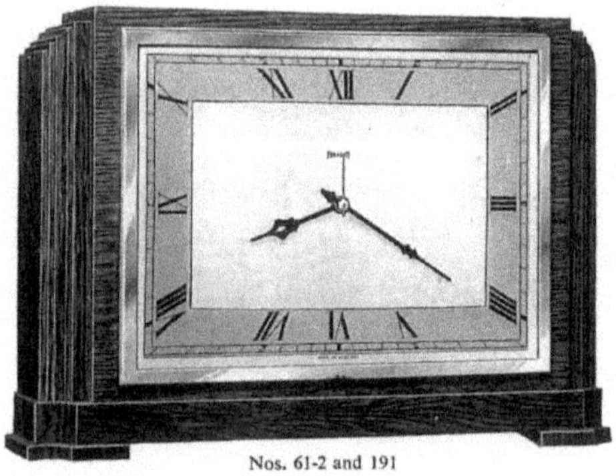

Nos. 61-2 and 191

MODEL No. 142. **Oak.** **82/6**

MODEL No. 143. **Walnut.** **92/6**

1938

8 in. × 6 in. Dial with Fret Silvered Zone, and **Chromium Bezel.**

Height, 8½ in. Width, 11½ in. Depth, 3½ in.

Nos. 142-3

MODEL No. 139. **Walnut.** **92/6**
With Ebonised Side Pieces.

8 in. × 6 in. Cream Dial with Silvered Zone, and **Chromium Bezel.**

Height, 7½ in. Width, 11 in. Depth, 3 in.

1938

No. 139

All images are courtesy of MOSI

No. 6. 3″ Cream Dial. 25/–
In Moulded Case, Walnut, Red Mahogany, and Blue Enamel finishes.

The FERRANTI Electric Alarm Clock has all the advantages of the ordinary FERRANTI Synchronous Electric Clock, but in addition is provided with a buzzer alarm, persistent without being strident.

The setting of the alarm is designed on a 24-hour basis and having once been set at any given time, **the alarm is arranged to function at that time once every twenty-four hours,** and when quietened **it does not require to be re-set for the following day.**

It is possible to put the alarm mechanism out of action if required.

1936

1936

ALARM CLOCK WITH AUTOMATICALLY CONTROLLED FLOODLIT DIAL

In addition to the special features of 24-hour setting and automatic re-set, as in the Model No. 6 FERRANTI Electric Alarm Clock, **the dial of the Model No. 7 is floodlit** through the medium of an ordinary 3½ volt flash-lamp bulb (easily replaceable) which is energised from the mains.

The light is automatically controlled to switch on at approximately 12 midnight and switch off at approximately 8 a.m.

A separate switch is provided to enable the light to be put off and on at will, during the **8 hours floodlighting period.**

No. 7. 3″ Cream Dial, raised Silvered Zone. 35/–
In Moulded Case, Walnut, Red Mahogany, and Blue Enamel finishes.

All images are courtesy of MOSI

MODEL No. 7 **35/-**

Electric Alarm Clock, with an automatically controlled Floodlit Dial.

3 in. Cream Dial,
Raised Silvered Zone.

In Moulded **Walnut or Mahogany** Cases, also Blue Enamel Finishes.

Height, 5¼ in. Width, 4¼ in. Depth, 2½ in.

1938

MODEL No. 9 **25/-**

3½ in. Cream Dial and
Raised Silvered Zone.

In Moulded **Walnut** Cases, also
Green or Blue Enamel Finishes.
(Other colours available at 7/6 extra.)

Height, 5¼ in. Width, 4½ in. Depth, 2½ in.

The FERRANTI Electric Alarm Clock is provided with a buzzer alarm, persistent without being strident.
The setting of the alarm is designed on a 24-hour basis and, having once been set at any given time, the alarm is arranged to function at that time once every 24 hours, and when quietened it does not require to be re-set for the following day.
It is possible to put the alarm mechanism out of action if required.

1938

All images are courtesy of MOSI

Alarm Clocks

ALARM CLOCK

1947

No. 947—Moulded case in Walnut, Pink and Blue finishes. 3″ tinted dial with Silvered zone.

This new Alarm Clock retains the usual FERRANTI feature of 24 hour setting, the buzzer alarm, having once been set, functions once every 24 hours, and when quietened does not require to be re-set for the following day.

The alarm control knob can be depressed and locked down if the alarm is not required to operate.

ALARM CLOCKS

1952

No. 947—Moulded case in Walnut and Green finishes. 3″ tinted dial with Silvered zone. This Alarm Clock retains the usual FERRANTI feature of 24 hour setting; the buzzer alarm, having once been set, functions once every 24 hours, and when quietened does not require to be re-set for the following day. The alarm control knob can be depressed and locked down if the alarm is not required to operate.

ALARM CLOCK

1955

No. 551 – Moulded Polystyrene case with Maroon, Green or Cream front and either Cream or Beige back. 4 in. Cream dial with embossed Gilt numerals. Gilt inner bezel. Luminous spots at the hours with larger luminous markings at 12, 3, 6 and 9 for easy identification in the dark. Luminous hands. This Alarm Clock retains the usual Ferranti feature of 24-hour setting; the buzzer alarm, having once been set, functions once every 24 hours, and when quietened does not require to be re-set for the following day. The alarm control knob can be depressed and locked down if the alarm is not required to operate.

1938

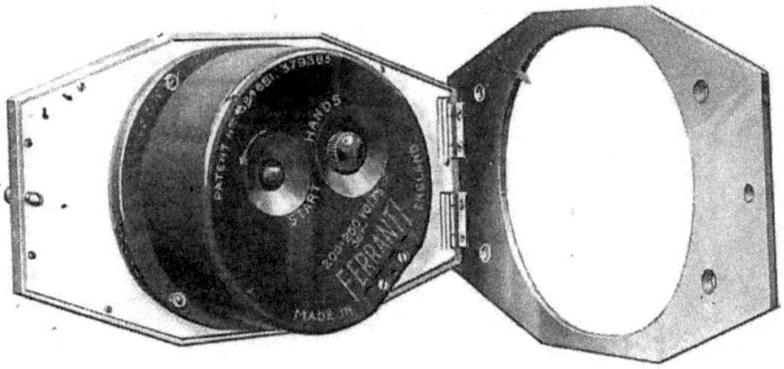

The above illustration shows the method of hinging applicable to Nos. 107, 108, 109, 110, 111, and 112.

Nos. 107, 108, 109, 110, 111, and 112 are available with either a silver or walnut inset dial, with raised zone and hinged frame. Each model consists of a clock drum movement complete with dial and chromium bezel, and is hinged to a metal backplate.

The movement is encased in a bakelite drum which projects behind the backplate $2\frac{1}{8}$". Diameter, $3\frac{3}{4}$". Depth, $2\frac{3}{4}$".

1938

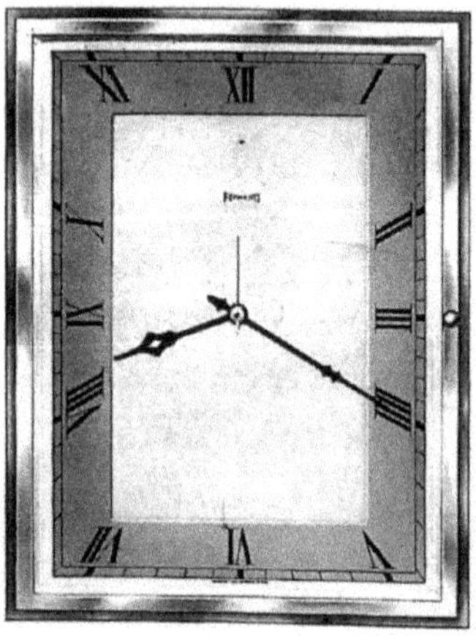

No. 107

MODEL No. 107 **52/6**

6 in. × 8 in. Cream Dial
with Silvered Zone.

Height, $8\frac{1}{2}$ in. Width, $6\frac{1}{2}$ in. Depth, $2\frac{1}{4}$ in.

1938

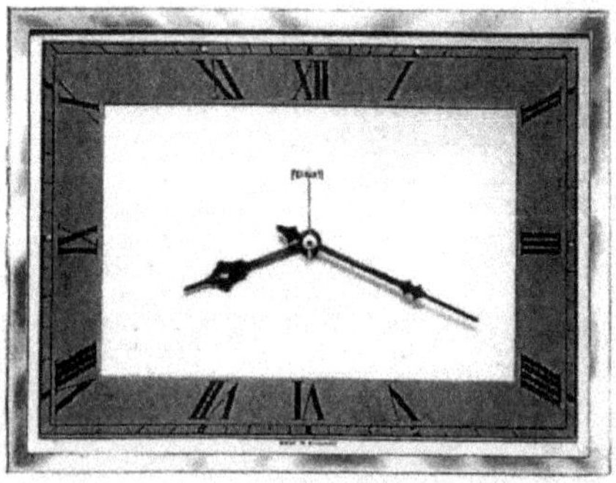

No. 108

MODEL No. 108 **52/6**

8 in. × 6 in. Cream Dial
with Silvered Zone.

Height, $6\frac{1}{2}$ in. Width, $8\frac{1}{2}$ in. Depth, $2\frac{1}{4}$ in.

All images are courtesy of MOSI

Flush Fitting Clocks

No. 109

MODEL No. 109 **50/-**

6 in. × 6 in. Cream Dial
with Silvered Zone.

Height, $6\frac{1}{2}$ in. Width, $6\frac{1}{2}$ in. Depth, $2\frac{1}{2}$ in.

1938

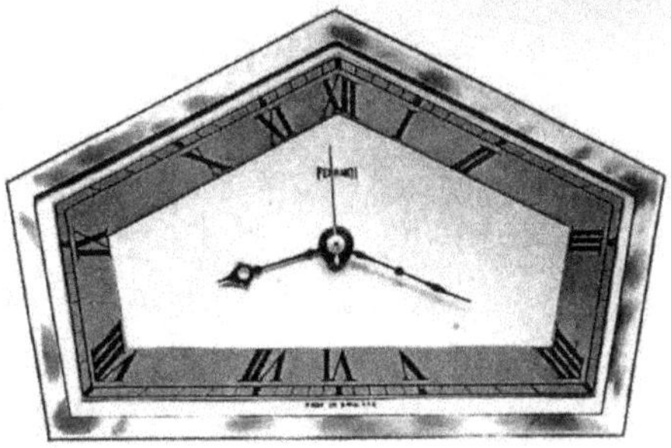

No. 110

MODEL No. 110 **50/-**

6 in. × 4 in. Cream Dial
with Silvered Zone.

Height, $4\frac{3}{4}$ in. Width, $7\frac{1}{2}$ in. Depth, $2\frac{1}{2}$ in.

1938

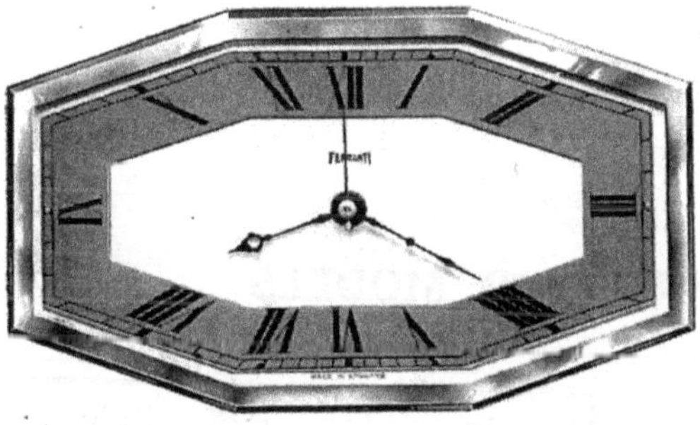

No. 111

MODEL No. 111 **45/-**

6 in. × $3\frac{1}{2}$ in. Cream Dial
with Silvered Zone.

Height, $4\frac{1}{2}$ in. Width, $7\frac{1}{2}$ in. Depth, $2\frac{1}{2}$ in.

1938

No. 112

MODEL No. 112 **52/6**

7 in. × 4 in. Cream Dial
with Silvered Zone.

Height, 6 in. Width, 8 in. Depth, $2\frac{3}{4}$ in.

1938

All images are courtesy of MOSI

Flush Fitting Clocks

No. 113

1938

No. 114

MODEL No. 113 **32/6**

$3\frac{1}{2}$ in. × $3\frac{1}{2}$ in. Cream Dial with Silvered Zone.

Overall, $4\frac{1}{4}$ in. square. Depth, $2\frac{3}{4}$ in.

MODEL No. 114 **30/-**

$3\frac{1}{2}$ in. Cream Dial with Silvered Zone.

Overall diameter, $3\frac{3}{4}$ in. Depth, $2\frac{3}{4}$ in.

Nos. 113 and 114 are provided with a Ball and Socket fixing arrangement. A Metal Casing is supplied with each movement for cementing or screwing into mantelpieces, or any other position where it is desired to mount the Clock.

Flush Mounting Type.

No. 128. Dial 10″ × 10″.
No. 129. Dial 15″ × 15″.

Price on application.

1934

INTERIOR MODELS

1936

FLUSH MOUNTING TYPE.

No. 128	... ... 10″ × 10″ Silvered Dial	... ...	**£10 10 0**
No. 129	... ... 12″ × 12″ Silvered Dial	... ...	**£13 0 0**

All images are courtesy of MOSI

Glass and Chrome Clocks

No. 118

1938

MODEL No. 118 **95/-**

4 in. Silvered Zone on Mirrored Ground with **Chromium** Base.

Available in Peach, Green and Amber.

Height, 7 in. Width 8¾ in. Depth, 2¾ in.

1938

MODEL No. 120 **110/-**

4 in. Silvered Zone on Mirrored Ground with **Chromium** Base.

Available in Peach, Green and Amber.

Height, 6 in. Width, 10 in. Depth, 2¾ in.

No. 120

1947

No. 294—Mirror glass on Chrome feet, with Cream, Green or Brown background. 5½" Bronze fretted zone.

1952

No. 299—Mirror glass and chrome with 6" Silvered zone. In Peach or Green.

MODEL No. 119 **100/-**

4 in. Silvered Zone on Mirrored Ground with **Chromium** Base.

Available in Peach, Green and Amber.

Height, 7 in. Width, 10¼ in. Depth, 3 in.

1938

No. 119

Grand Daughter Clocks

1936 Models

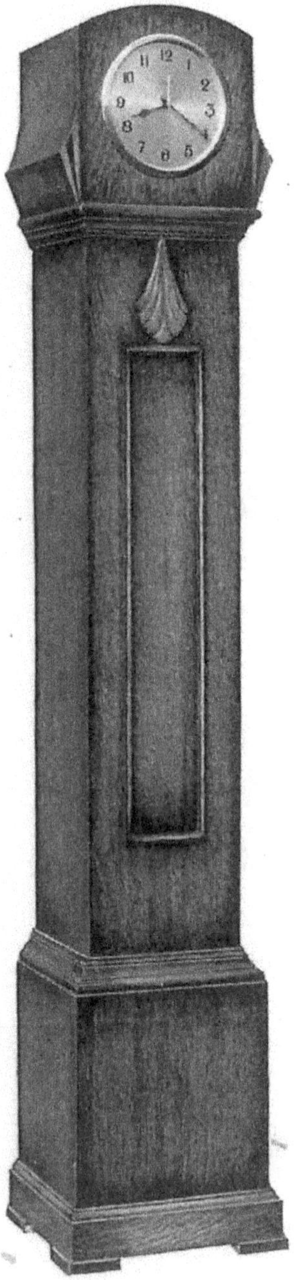

No. 150. 99/6
Jacobean Oak Case, 6″ Silvered Dial, Chromium Bezel.

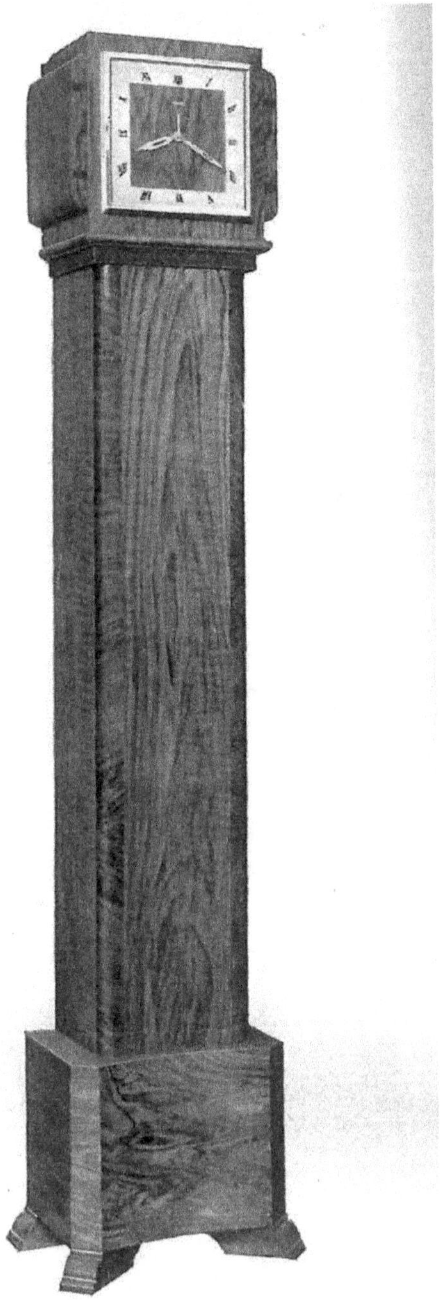

No. 151. 195/-
A Modern Grand-daughter in Figured Walnut Case, Natural Wood Dial, 7″ × 7″ Raised Silvered Zone, Chromium Bezel.

All images are courtesy of MOSI

Grand Daughter Clocks

1938 and Later

SQUARE TYPES

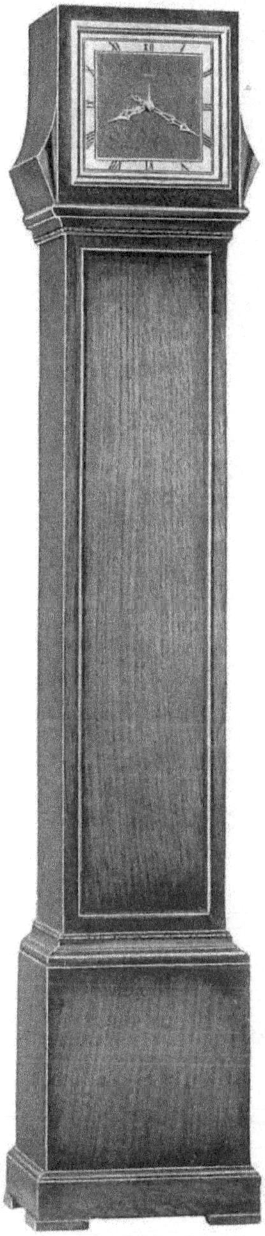

MODEL No. 150 **Timepiece.** **105/-**

Strike. **130/-**

Chime. **168/-**

Square **Oak** Case.

7 in. Square Dial with Raised Zone, and **Chromium Bezel.**

Height, 4 ft. 6 in. Width, 10¼ in. Depth, 8¼ in.

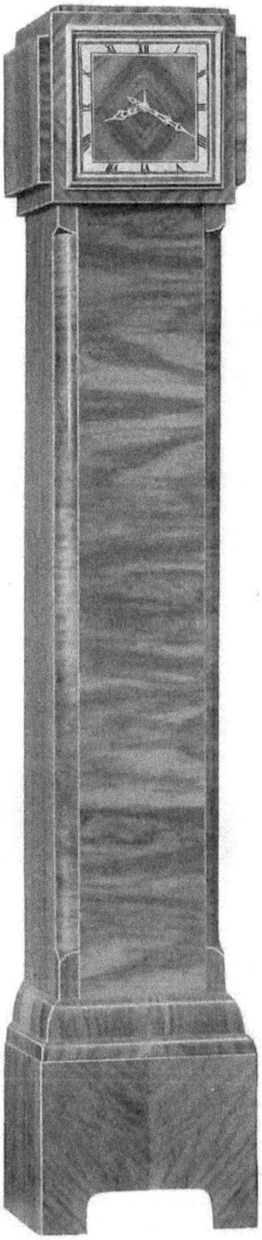

MODEL No. 151 **Timepiece.** **145/-**

Strike. **175/-**

Square **Walnut** Case.

7 in. Square Dial with Raised Zone, and **Chromium Bezel.**

Height, 4 ft. 6 in. Width. 10 in. Depth, 8¼in.

All images are courtesy of MOSI

1938 and later

CORNER TYPES

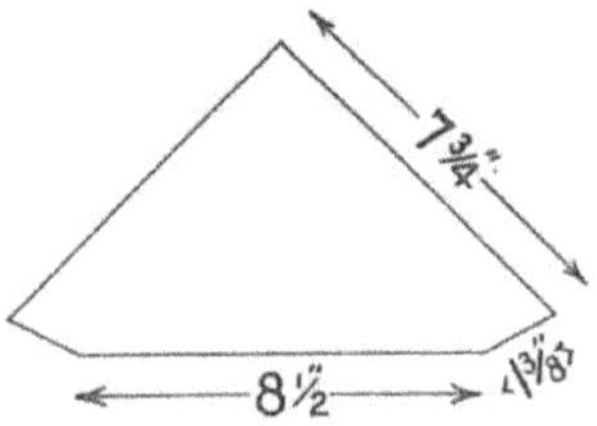

SECTION.

MODEL No. 152 **Timepiece.** **135/-**

Strike. **165/-**

Corner **Oak** Case.

7 in. Square Dial with Raised Zone, and **Chromium Bezel.**

Height, 4 ft. 7 in. Width, 11½ in. Depth, 7½ in.

MODEL No. 153 **Timepiece.** **160/-**

Strike. **190/-**

Corner **Walnut** Case.

7 in. Square Dial with Raised Zone, and **Chromium Bezel.**

Height, 4 ft. 6 in. Width, 11 in. Depth, 7½ in.

Page 27

All images are courtesy of MOSI

Moulded Case Clocks

1936

No. 1. 3½″ Silvered Dial. 30/-

1936

No. 2. 3½″ Silvered Dial. 30/-

No. 4. 3½″ Silvered Dial. 35/-

1936

Models Nos. 1, 2, 3, and 4 are available in beautiful Bakelite Cases finished in Walnut, Mahogany, Black, Mottled Red, Blue Enamel, and Green Enamel.

No. 3. 3½″ Silvered Dial. 30/-

1936

No. 3

MODEL No. 3 30/-

3½ in. Dial.

Moulded Cases in **Walnut**, **Mahogany**, and Black, also Blue and Green enamels.

Height, 6 in. Width, 6 in. Depth, 2¾ in.

1938

Moulded Case Clocks

1938

MODEL No. 5 **32/6**

$3\frac{1}{2}$ in. Dial.

In moulded **Walnut** or **Mahogany** cases.
Chromium Bezel.

Height, $6\frac{1}{4}$ in. Width, 7 in.
Depth, $3\frac{3}{4}$ in.

No. 5

1947

No. 8—Moulded Walnut case.
$3\frac{1}{2}''$ Cream dial.

No. 5. $3\frac{1}{2}''$ Silvered Dial. **35/-**
In beautiful Walnut or Mahogany Moulded Case, Chromium Bezel.

1936

No. 8. 23/6

$3\frac{1}{2}''$ Cream Dial.
Raised Silvered Zone.
In Moulded Case.
Walnut or Mahogany Finish.

Height ... ... $5\frac{3}{4}''$
Width ... ... $4\frac{3}{4}''$
Depth ... ... $2\frac{3}{8}''$

1936

MODEL No. 8 **23/6**

$3\frac{1}{2}$ in. Cream Dial.

Raised Silvered Zone, and
Chromium Bezel.
In moulded
Walnut or **Mahogany cases.**

Height, $5\frac{3}{4}$ in. Width, $4\frac{3}{4}$ in.
Depth, $2\frac{1}{2}$ in.

1938

No. 8 *Page 5*

All images are courtesy of MOSI

Moulded Case Clocks

No. 10—Moulded Walnut case. 3½″ Cream dial. Also in Ivory, Green and Blue finishes.

1947

No. 11—Moulded Walnut case. 3½″Cream dial. Also in Ivory, Green and Blue finishes.

1947

No. 12—Moulded Walnut case. 3½″ Cream dial. Also in Ivory, Green and Blue finishes.

1952

No. 14—Moulded Cream case. 4″ dial with Silvered zone. Also in Green and Blue.

1952

All images are courtesy of MOSI

Moulded Case Clocks

1952

No. 15—Moulded Cream case with 4″ dial and Silvered zone. Also in Green and Blue.

1952

No. 16—Moulded Ivory case. 3½″ Cream dial. Silvered zone. Also in Green and Blue.

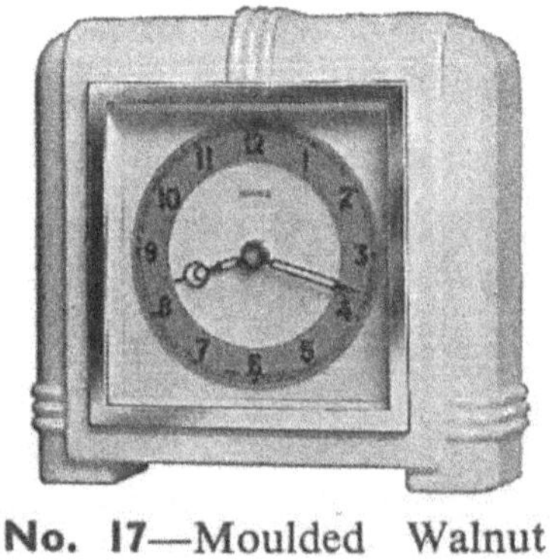

No. 17—Moulded Walnut or Ivory case. 3½″ Cream dial.

1952

All images are courtesy of MOSI

1938

No. 70

MOVEMENTS

MODEL No. 70.
45/-

6 in. Cream Dial and Silvered Zone.

Bakelite Drum Movement.

Chromium Bezel.

No. 30 (Illus.) **30/-**
No. 30a (Sq. Dial) **32/6**

$3\frac{1}{2}$ in. Cream Dial. Bakelite Drum Movement. **Chromium Bezel.** Complete with fixing ring and chromium-plated cover plate, suitable for replacing unreliable spring-driven Movements.

1938

No. 30

1938

No. 80

No. 80 (illus.) **30/-**
No. 80a (sq. Dial) **32/6**

$3\frac{1}{2}$ in. Cream Dial. Bakelite Drum Movement. **Chromium Bezel.** Complete with two clips for panel mounting. Panel hole should be $3\frac{11}{16}$ in. Flexible lead not supplied.

MODEL No. 50. **30/-**

Suitable for dials up to $\frac{3}{32}$ in. thick.

MODEL No. 50a. **32/6**

Suitable for dials up to $\frac{1}{4}$ in. thick.

These Movements are designed to replace Movements in existing Clocks having dial sizes of not more than 12 in. diameter, utilising the existing dial and hands. Complete with set of two hand collets.

1936

Nos. 50-50a

1934

No. 80. **30/-**
This Clock has been produced specially for fitting into the front panel of an A.C. Mains Radio Receiver. It has a Chromium Bezel and $3\frac{1}{2}''$ dial. Two clips are provided to facilitate fixing without the use of screws. Panel hole should be $3\frac{11}{16}''$. Flexible cord not supplied with this model.

Nos. 30, 50, and 80 will only be supplied for the specific purpose indicated, and will not be supplied for fitting into clock cases intended for re-sale.

1934

No. 30. **30/-**
Bakelite Drum Movement,
Chromium Bezel, $3\frac{1}{2}''$ dial.
Movement only, designed to fit $3\frac{1}{2}''$ movement case, so that if an unreliable spring-driven movement is fitted in an existing case it may be removed and replaced by the Ferranti Electric Clock movement quite easily.

No. 50. **30/-**
This Movement is specially designed to replace movements in existing clocks of large sizes up to and including 12″ dials, and has a specially lengthened and strengthened centre arbor. It includes a moulded Bakelite terminal cover and a length of flexible cord.

1934

Ornate Clocks

1934

No. 11. **45/-**

Oxydised Silver, Chromium Bezel, 3½″ dial.

1934

No. 12. **63/-**

Untarnishable Talbot Pewter, Chromium Bezel, 3½″ dial.

The hand hammering of the ancient craftsman has been faithfully reproduced in this Model thereby lending charm and distinction to modern schemes of decoration and furnishing.

MODEL No. 104 75/-

Ebonised Case and Strappings.
Mirror Glass front.
3½ in. Cream Dial with Silvered Zone.

Height, 6½ in. Width, 8¾ in. Depth, 3¼ in.

1938

No. 104

MODEL No. 117 **37/6**

Chromium Finish.
3½ in. Cream Dial with Silvered Zone.

Height, 5½ in. Width, 5⅞ in. Depth, 2½ in.

1938

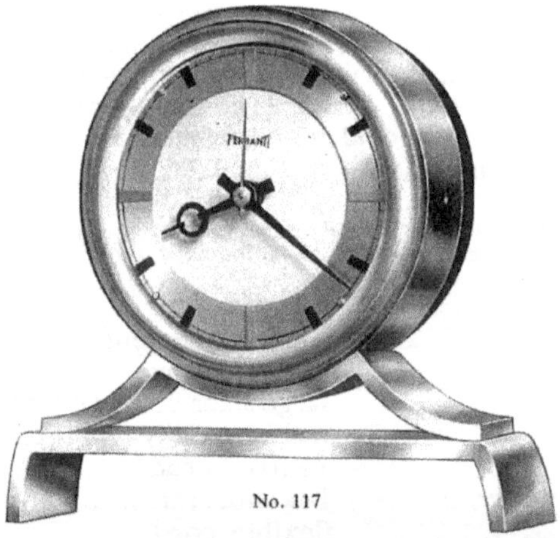

No. 117

All images are courtesy of MOSI

Model No. 243. **49/6**

Octagonal fretted copper zone and copper hands, green and chromium base. 5″ green anodized dial.

ALTERNATIVE FINISH :

Chromium base and zone with cream dial.

Height 5¾″. Width 5¼″. Depth 3″.

1938

Model No. 241. **45/-**

Semi-circular briolite panel, in blue, green, or amber, chromium and briolite plinths. 3½″ silvered fret zone and chromium bezel.

Height 5″. Width 9″. Depth 3½″.

1938

Model No. 240. **40/-**

Coloured briolite panel in blue, green, or amber, with chromium base.

3½″ silvered fret zone and chromium bezel.

Height 5¾″. Width 6″. Depth 3″.

1938

1938

Model No. 242. **42/6**

Coloured catalin panel in pink or green with chromium supports. 3½″ circular silvered fret zone and chromium bezel.

Height 5½″. Width 7½″. Depth 3″.

1938

Model No. 244. 56/-
Mottled green celastoid dial, chromium hair-line bezel. Black and chromium base. 6" dial with silvered zone.
Height 8". Width 7".
Depth 3".

No. 288—$5\frac{1}{2}$" Ivory Plastic dial, with Black base.

1947

1938

Model No. 245. 85/-
Real green onyx dial covered with plate glass face. Additional cover glass over the hands. Ebonised and chromium base. 6" dial with figures printed on plate glass.
Height $8\frac{1}{2}$". Width $8\frac{1}{2}$".
Depth $3\frac{1}{2}$".

1938

Model No. 249. Oak. 60/-
Model No. 250. Walnut. 63/-
The dial of this clock is recessed and the face covered with plate glass upon which the figures are printed. Clock supported by chromium and ebony plinths. Silver girder type hands.
Depth, 3".
Height $6\frac{1}{2}$". Width $8\frac{3}{4}$".

All images are courtesy of MOSI

Ornate Clocks

No. 290—Transparent tinted panel in Pink or Green. 4½″ Silvered zone.

1952

No. 292—Mirror glass with Satin Silver dial. 5″ tinted zone.

1952

No. 293—Mirror glass with 5″ tinted dial on Cream, Green or Brown background.

1952

No. 294—Mirror glass on Chrome feet, with Cream, Green or Brown background. 5½″ Bronze fretted zone.

1952

All images are courtesy of MOSI

No. 295 1952

No. 296 1952

$3\frac{1}{2}$ in. – $4\frac{1}{4}$ in. DIALS

No. 296 – Coloured Perspex panel on Chromium-plated base. Cream, Green or Blue. $3\frac{1}{2}$ in. Black zone with Silver numerals. Black hands.

No. 295 – Coloured Perspex panel on Chromium-plated base. Cream, Green or Blue. 4 in. slotted Chromium-plated zone. Black hands.

No. 297 – Transparent tinted Perspex panel in Pink, Green or Blue with Chromium-plated feet. 4in. Silvered zone with Black Roman numerals. Black hands.

No. 553 – Grained Brass with clear Perspex panel. $4\frac{1}{4}$ in. dial with Spun Gilt centre and Gilt numerals on Black background. Black hands.

No. 297 1952

No. 553 1955

Ornate Clocks

No. 552

1955

No. 552 – Grained Brass with Black base. $5\frac{3}{4}$ in. Dial. Gilt fretted zone on circular grained Silver background.

No. 299 – Mirror glass with Chromium-plated base and side clips. 6 in. circular grained Silver dial with Black Roman numerals. Chromium-plated hands. In Peach or Green.

No. 299

All images are courtesy of MOSI

Shaped Dial Mantel Clocks

No. 56. **84/-**
Art Walnut Case, Chromium Bezel.

1934

No. 65.	Oak.	**84/-**
No. 66.	Mahogany.	**90/-**
No. 67.	Walnut.	**90/-**

Dial 7″ × 4″.
Chromium Bezel.

1934

MODEL No. 91. **Oak.**	67/6
MODEL No. 92. **Limed Oak.**	70/-
MODEL No. 93. **Walnut.**	80/-
MODEL No. 94. **Mahogany.**	75/-

6 in. × 3½ in. Cream Dial with Silvered Zone, and **Chromium Bezel.**

Height, 5¼ in. Width, 9¼ in.
Depth, 3¼ in.

1938

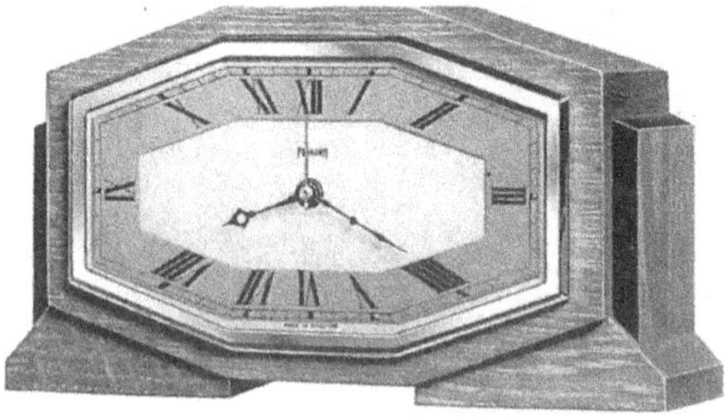

Nos. 91-2-3-4

No. 71.	Oak.	**67/6**
No. 72.	Mahogany.	**70/-**
No. 73.	Walnut.	**72/6**

Dial 6″ × 3½″.
Chromium Bezel.

1934

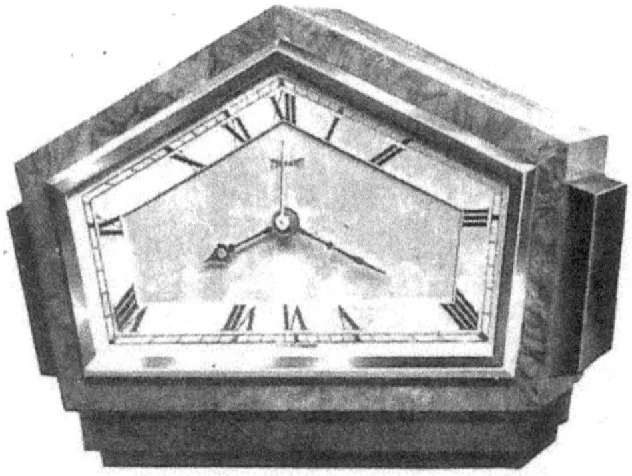

No. 81.	Oak.	**70/6**
No. 82.	Mahogany.	**72/6**
No. 83.	Walnut.	**80/-**
No. 84.	Burr Walnut.	**90/-**

Dial 6″ × 4″.
Chromium Bezel.

1934

All images are courtesy of MOSI

Shaped Dial Mantel Clocks

Nos. 133-4

MODEL No. 133. **Oak.** **84/-**

MODEL No. 134. **Walnut.** **90/-**

7 in. × 4 in. Cream Dial with Silvered Zone, and **Chromium Bezel.**

Height, 7¼ in. Width, 11¼ in. Depth, 3½ in.

1938

No. 135. **92/6**

Burr Walnut inlaid with Zebrano and Macassar.

7″ × 4″ Silvered Dial, Chromium Bezel.

1936

Nos 175-6

MODEL No. 175. **Oak.** **60/-**

MODEL No. 176. **Walnut.** **65/-**

6 in. × 4 in. Cream Dial and Silvered Zone, with **Chromium Bezel.**

Height 5¾ in. Width, 8 in. Depth, 3½ in.

1938

All images are courtesy of MOSI

Nos. 144-5

MODEL No. 144. **Oak.** **95/-**

MODEL No. 145. **Walnut.** **105/-**

6 in. Dial with Raised Silvered Zone, and **Chromium Bezel.**

Height, 8 in. Width, 9¼ in. Depth, 3¼ in.

Striking Model only.

1936

MODEL No. 146. **Oak.** **65/-**

6 in. Dial with Fret Silvered Zone, and **Chromium Bezel.**

Height, 7¾ in. Width, 8 in. Depth, 3¼ in.

Striking Model only.

1938

No. 146

Nos. 147-8 (Striking Models). Nos. 185-6 (Chiming Models).

STRIKING MODELS.

MODEL No. 147. **Oak.** **100/-**

MODEL No. 148. **Walnut.** **110/-**

CHIMING MODELS.

MODEL No. 185. **Oak.** **125/-**

MODEL No. 186. **Walnut.** **150/-**

8 in. × 6 in. Dial with Raised Silvered Zone, and **Chromium Bezel.**

Height, 8 in. Width, 10 in. Depth, 3 in.

Depth of Chiming Model, 4¼ in.

1938

All images are courtesy of MOSI

No. 149

STRIKING MODEL.

MODEL No. 180. **Walnut.** **85/-**

CHIMING MODEL.

MODEL No. 149. **Walnut.** **126/-**

6 in. Dial with Fret Silvered Zone, and **Chromium Bezel.**

Height, 8¾ in. Width, 11¼ in. Depth, 3 in.
Depth of Chiming Model, 4¼ in.

1938

Nos. 181-2

MODEL No. 181. **Oak.** **90/-**

MODEL No. 182. **Walnut.** **105/-**

6 in. Dial with Silvered Fret Zone, and **Chromium Bezel.**

Height, 8 in. Width, 10 in. Depth, 3¼ in.
Striking Model only.

1938

1934

No. 95. With Base. **67/6**
No. 115. Without Base. **52/6**
Dial 8″ × 6″.

No. 101. With Base. **67/6**
No. 118. Without Base. **52/6**
Dial 7″ × 4″.

1934

No. 97

1938

MODEL No. 97 **52/6**

Chromium Plated with **Ebony** Base.
8 in. × 6 in. Cream Dial with Silvered Zone.

Height, 6¾ in. Width, 10 in. Depth, 2½ in.

1934

No. 99. Timepiece, with base **60/–**
No. 117. Timepiece, without base **47/6**
No. 100. Alarm, with base. **70/–**
No. 96. Alarm, without base. **57/6**
Dial 6″ × 6″.

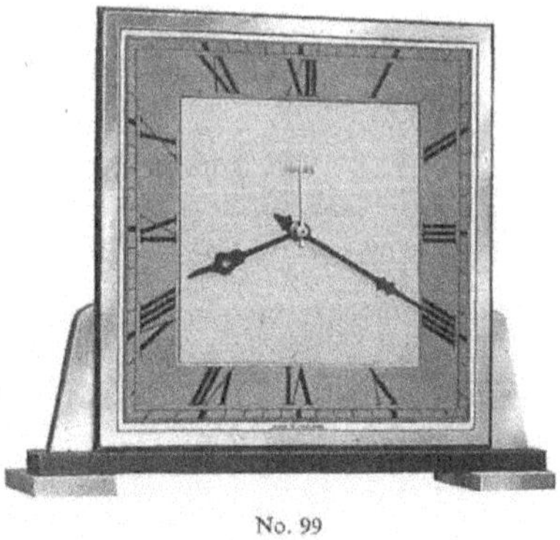

No. 99

MODEL No. 99 50/-

Chromium Plated with **Ebony** Base.
6 in. × 6 in. Cream Dial with Silvered Zone.

Height, 6¾ in. Width, 8 in. Depth, 2½ in.

1938

All images are courtesy of MOSI

Strut Clocks

No. 105.	Timepiece, with base.	**55/–**
No. 120	Timepiece, without base.	**42/6**
No. 106.	Alarm, with base.	**65/–**
No. 102.	Alarm, without base,	**52/6**
	Dial 6″ × $3\frac{1}{2}$″.	

No. 103.	Timepiece, with base.	**57/6**
No. 119.	Timepiece, without base.	**45/–**
No. 104.	Alarm, with base.	**67/6**
No. 98.	Alarm, without base.	**55/–**
	Dial 6″ × 4″.	

1934

MODEL No. 105 **45/-**

Chromium Plated with **Ebony** Base.
6 in. × $3\frac{1}{2}$ in. Cream Dial with Silvered Zone.

Height, $4\frac{3}{4}$ in. Width, $6\frac{3}{4}$ in. Depth, $2\frac{1}{2}$ in.

1938

No. 105

No. 103

1938

MODEL No. 103 **50/-**

Chromium Plated with **Ebony** Base.
6 in. × 4 in. Cream Dial with Silvered Zone.

Height, 5 in. Width, $7\frac{3}{4}$ in. Depth, $2\frac{1}{2}$ in.

1936 and later

MODEL No. 100 **32/6**

$3\frac{1}{2}$ in. Cream Dial with Silvered Zone, and **Chromium Finish.**

Height, $4\frac{3}{4}$ in. Width, $6\frac{1}{2}$ in. Depth, $2\frac{1}{4}$ in.

No. 100

All images are courtesy of MOSI

1938

No. 115

MODEL No. 115 63/-

Chromium Finish.
6 in. Cream Dial with
Silvered Zone.

Height, $6\frac{3}{4}$ in. Width, $8\frac{3}{4}$ in. Depth, $2\frac{1}{2}$ in.

1938

No. 116

MODEL No. 116 70/-

Chromium Finish.
5 in. × 5 in. Cream Dial with
Silvered Zone.

Height, $6\frac{1}{2}$ in. Width, $7\frac{3}{4}$ in. Depth, 3 in.

All images are courtesy of MOSI

Electric Stop Clock

1934

ELECTRIC STOP CLOCK.

No. 200. 6″ dial.

Black and Nickel Case. Dial Cream Enamel. For timing operations with accuracy of 1/20th part of a second. If required, larger dials can be supplied.

Price on application.

All images are courtesy of MOSI

1938

Nos. 20-1-2-6

MODEL No. 20. 8 in. Dial.
Overall diam., 9½ in. Depth, 3 in. **52/6**

MODEL No. 21. 10 in. Dial.
Overall diam., 11½ in. Depth, 3 in. **55/-**

MODEL No. 22. 12 in. Dial.
Overall diam., 13½ in. Depth, 3 in. **57/6**

MODEL No. 26. 18 in. Dial.
Overall diam., 21 in. Depth, 3 in. **97/6**

1938

Nos. 18-9

MODEL No. 18. 12 in. Dials. **145/-**

MODEL No. 19. 18 in. Dials. **220/-**

Double Sided
and fitted with two hooks
for Chain Suspension.

Cream Enamel Dial, Metal Case, Standard Finish Oxy-Copper. All Clocks illustrated with Front Setting and Starting Control.

Model No.23 -1934- same as 22 but back starting)

Model No. 22,26,18,19 - 1936 - available with Cream or Black enamel dial and Arabic or Roman numerals

1936

No. 25. **50/–**
6″ WALL CLOCK, Silvered Dial, Metal Case, standard finish Oxy-Copper. Also available in Chromium Plate, Black, White, or Brown Enamel to order, at no extra.

No. 24. Solid Oak **£6 12 6**
24a Solid Walnut **£7 15 0**

12″ Wall Clock in beautifully finished octagonal wood case, with Chromium frame and Cream Enamel Dial, fitted with side setting and starting control.

1934

All images are courtesy of MOSI

WALL CLOCKS

1955

No. 20 – 8 in. dial.
No. 21 – 10 in. dial.
No. 22 – 12 in. dial.
No. 26 – 18 in. dial.

Matt White dial in spun Aluminium case. Standard finish Metallic Bronze. Special finishes to order.

DOUBLE SIDED SUSPENSION CLOCKS

No. 18 – 12 in. dials.
No. 19 – 18 in. dials.

Finish as above. These clocks are fitted with two hooks for chain suspension.

No. 189 – 10 in. square dial in Walnut veneered case with inlaid Sycamore chaplets and exposed Gilt hands.

No. 28 – Moulded case in Cream, Green or Blue finish. 6 in. dial with Brown figures and hands.

No. 20, No. 2
No. 22, No. 26

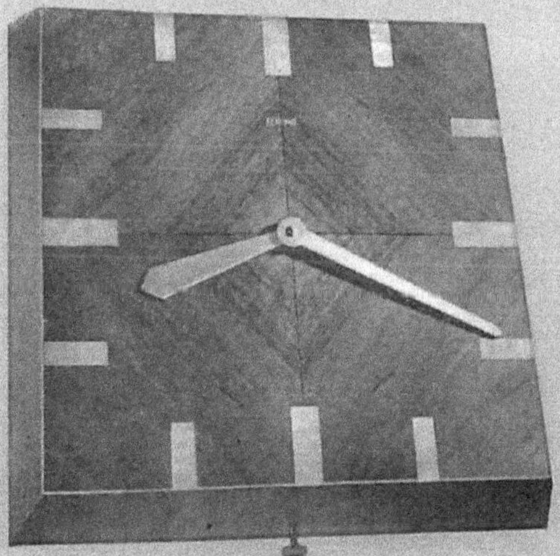

No. 189

No. 28

All images are courtesy of MOSI

Wall Clocks

WALL MODEL

No. 27. 25/-

5″ Cream Dial.
In Moulded Case.
Walnut or Mahogany
or
Cream Enamel Finish.

Height	... ...	8″
Width	... ...	8″
Depth	... ...	2¾″

1936

1938

No. 27

MODEL No. 27 **25/-**

In Moulded **Walnut** Case, also
Green, Blue, or Cream Enamel Finish.
5 in. Cream Dial and
Raised Silvered Zone.

Height, 8 in. Width, 8 in. Depth, 2¾ in.

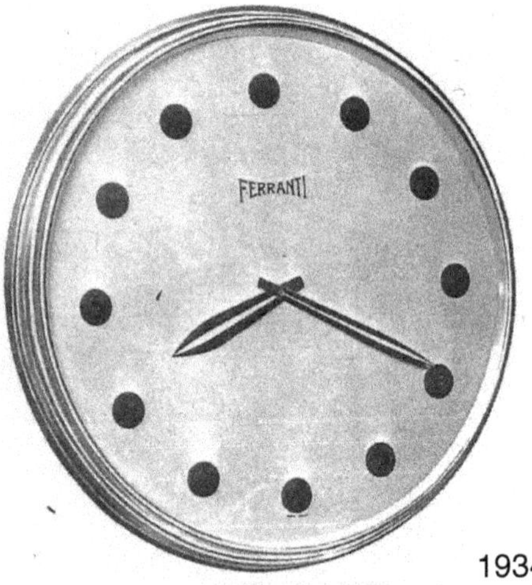

1934

WALL CLOCK. Special Type.
No. 27. 18″ Dial. **£7 10 0.**
Antique Brass or Chromium Plated Case. Side setting. When ordering, please specify colour of hands and motifs.

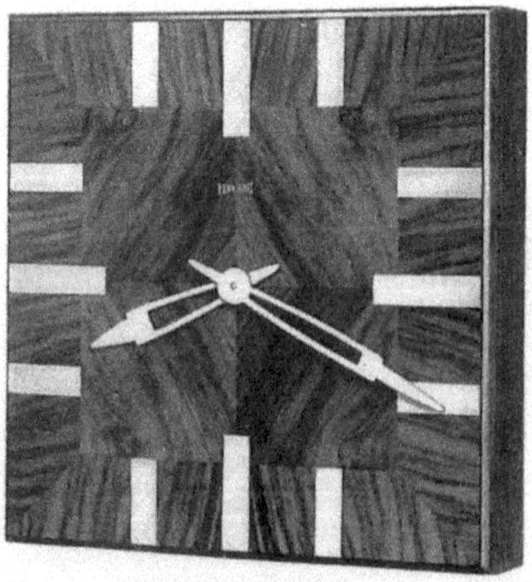

No. 189

MODEL No. 189 **65/-**

Walnut Case,
with Inlaid **Sycamore** Chaplets
and Brass Hands.
Bottom Starting Control.

Height, 12¼ in. Width, 12¼ in. Depth, 3 in.

1938

All images are courtesy of MOSI

Wall Clocks

1934

No. 28. **£8 2 6**

With illumination from top only.
Dial size, 10″ × 14″.

No. 29. **£10 15 0**

With illumination from top and bottom.
Dial size, 18″ × 14″.
(*As illustrated.*)

These models can be supplied with customers' own advertising matter at the above prices.

No. 28 requires one tubular lamp and No. 29 requires two tubular lamps (30 watts). Price approximately 4/- each.

1947 and later

No. 28—Moulded case. Walnut finish with raised Gilt figures and Gilt hands. 6″ dial. Also in Ivory, Green or Blue.

1938

No. 29

MODEL No. 29 **50/-**

In Moulded **Walnut** Case, also Green and Cream Enamel Finish. 6 in. Cream Dial with Silvered Zone and **Chromium Bezel.** Moulded Bakelite Case.

Height, 8¾ in. Width, 8¾ in. Depth, 2¾ in.

All images are courtesy of MOSI

1938

Nos. 121-2-3

MODEL No. 121. 8 in. Dial. **62/6**
Overall diameter, 9½ in. Depth, 3 in.

MODEL No. 122. 10 in. Dial. **67/6**
Overall diameter, 11½ in. Depth, 3 in.

MODEL No. 123. 12 in. Dial. **72/6**
Overall diameter, 13½ in. Depth, 3 in.

Single-sided Wall Clock
in **Chromium** Plated Case.

1938

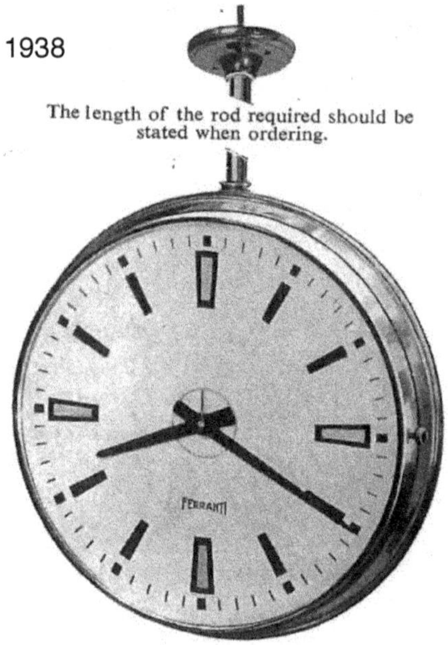

Nos. 125-6-7

MODEL No. 125. 8 in. Dial. **155/-**
Overall diameter, 9½ in. Depth, 6 in.

MODEL No. 126. 10 in. Dial. **165/-**
Overall diameter, 11½ in. Depth, 6 in.

MODEL No. 127. 12 in. Dial. **177/6**
Overall diameter, 13½ in. Depth, 6 in.

Double-sided Suspension Clock
in **Chromium** Plated Case.

Nos. 128-9

MODEL No. 128 **210/-**
10 in. Square Dial.
Height, 11¼ in. Depth, 2¾ in. Width, 11¼ in.

MODEL No. 129 **260/-**
12 in. Square Dial.
Height, 13¼ in. Width, 13¼ in. Depth, 2¾ in.
Flush mounting.
Cream Dial with Silvered Zone, and
Chromium Bezel.

1938

No. 124. 12″ Dial. **£11 15 0**
Carved Walnut. Bronze Rim.

1934

All images are courtesy of MOSI

No. 187

MODEL No. 187 **95/-**

Circular **Oak** Case, with
Brass Roman Numerals and Hands.
Bottom Starting Control.

Overall diameter, 15 in. Depth, 3 in.

1938

No. 188

MODEL No. 188 **95/-**

Walnut Case, with
Brass Arabic Numerals and Hands.
Bottom Starting Control.

Height, 13 in. Width, 13 in. Depth, 2¾ in.

1938

No. 190

MODEL No. 190 **110/-**

Octagonal **Walnut** Case,
with Brass Chaplets and Hands.

Bottom Starting Control.

Height, 14 in Width, 14 in. Depth, 3½ in.

1938

All images are courtesy of MOSI

No. 217. Cinema type Clock on wood panel, 20″ × 22″. Walnut or Mahogany finish. 18″ Dial. Illumination from top. Side setting and starting control. **£8 10 0**

No. 218. (*Illustrated*). Cinema type Clock on wood panel, 20″ × 36″, with space for advertising matter, 18″ × 13″. Walnut or Mahogany finish. 18″ Dial. Illumination top or bottom of Panel. Side setting and starting control. **£10 10 0**

SPECIAL TYPES OF ADVERTISING

1936

Nos. 219-20

MODEL No. 219.		18 in. Dial.	**240/-**
Height, 25 in.	Width, 25 in.		Depth, 4 in.
MODEL No. 220.		24 in. Dial.	**357/-**
Height, 31 in.	Width, 31 in.		Depth, 5½ in.

Solid **Oak** Case, Opal Glass Dial with Black Motifs and Hands. Hands exposed. Illuminated behind Dial (4 lampholders). Side Setting and Starting Control.

Without Lamps.

1938

All images are courtesy of MOSI

Exterior Wall Clocks

Modern design single-sided Outdoor Clocks, for Wall mounting, in Cast Metal Case, standard finish Black Enamel. Illuminated Models have Opal Dial, Non-illuminated types Metal Dial, Cream-enamelled finish. Black motifs and black hands with white centres. Cover glass over dial. Illuminated Models have separate circuits for Clock and lighting.

SINGLE SIDED, SUITABLE FOR WALL MOUNTING.

No. 201.	18″.	Non Illuminated	£6 17 6.	*Ex Works.*
No. 202.	18″.	Illuminated	£13 17 6.	*Ex Works.*
No. 203.	24″.	Non Illuminated	£7 17 6.	*Ex Works.*
No. 204.	24″.	Illuminated	£15 10 0.	*Ex Works.*

1936

Double-sided Outdoor Models for Wall, or Pole mounting. Specifications as above

1936

DOUBLE SIDED, FOR WALL OR POLE MOUNTING.

No. 205.	18″.	Non Illuminated	£15 15 0.	*Ex Works.*
No. 206.	18″.	Illuminated	£18 18 0.	*Ex Works.*
No. 207.	24″.	Non Illuminated	£18 0 0.	*Ex Works.*
No. 208.	24″.	Illuminated	£21 0 0.	*Ex Works.*

The above Models are available with alternative designs of Dials and Hands if required.

1936

OUT-DOOR MODELS

Attractive design, available with Single or Double Dials. In Welded Steel Case, standard finish Black Enamel. Illuminated models have Opal Dials, Non-illuminated types Metal Dials, Cream-enamelled finish.

Black Numerals and Black Hands.

Illuminated Clocks contain Lampholders behind dials and have separate circuits for Clock and lighting.

No. 209.	18″.	Double-sided.	Illuminated (*Illustrated*) ...	£22 17 6.	*Ex Works.*
No. 210.	24″.	Double-sided.	Illuminated	£23 10 0.	*Ex Works.*
No. 211.	18″.	Single-sided.	Non-illuminated	£6 17 6.	*Ex Works.*
No. 212.	18″.	Single-sided.	Illuminated	£13 17 6.	*Ex Works.*
No. 213.	24″.	Single-sided.	Non-illuminated	£7 17 6.	*Ex Works.*
No. 214.	24″.	Single-sided.	Illuminated	£15 10 0.	*Ex Works.*

Exterior Wall Clocks

Nos. 209-10-11-12-13-14

No. 209. 18 in. Illuminated Dial, double-sided. **650/-**
Height, 24 in. Width, 33¼ in. Depth, 10¼ in.

No. 210. 24 in. Illuminated Dial, double-sided. **688/-**
Height, 27¾ in. Width, 37 in. Depth, 10¼ in.

No. 211. 18 in. Non-illuminated Dial, single-sided. **250/-**
Height, 24 in. Width, 24 in. Depth, 4 in.

No. 212. 18 in. Illuminated Dial, single-sided. **260/-**
Height, 24 in. Width, 24 in. Depth, 7 in.

No. 213. 24 in. Non-illuminated Dial, single-sided. **248/-**
Height, 27¾ in. Width, 27¾ in. Depth, 4 in.

No. 214. 24 in. Illuminated Dial, single-sided. **280/-**
Height, 27¾ in. Width, 27¾ in. Depth, 7 in.

(Models 211, 212, 213, 214 without Brackets, but with Fixing Lugs for Wall Mounting.)

1938

Nos. 215-16.

No. 215. 18 in. Double-sided, Illuminated. **£38 4 0**
Height, 31½ in. Width, 31¾ in. Depth, 10¼ in.

No. 216. 24 in. Double-sided, Illuminated. **£40 4 0**
Height, 38¾ in. Width, 37 in. Depth, 10¼ in.

All images are courtesy of MOSI

Ferranti Plug and Socket System

FERRANTI FUSED PLUG AND SAFETY SOCKETS

Standard TWO-PIN FERRANTI PLUG, with two ½-amp. Fuses and two spares **2/-**

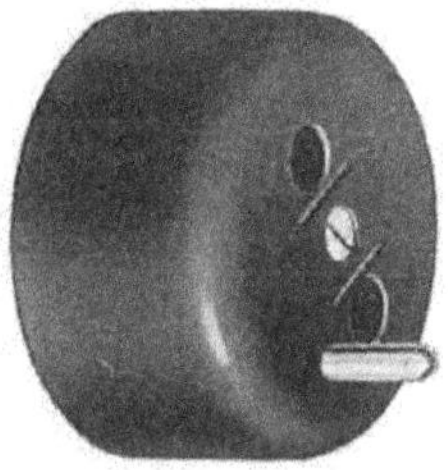

Projecting type SOCKET with Projecting Pin .. **10d.**

Flush-mounting SOCKET with Projecting Pin .. **1/4**

The FERRANTI Fused Plug is fitted internally with two small, easily replaceable Cartridge Fuses, which blow at 0·5 amp., and two spare Fuses are accommodated in the plug base. It fits any standard B.S.S. 5-amp. socket.

Replacement Cartridge Fuses available at 3/- per dozen.

1936

All images are courtesy of MOSI

Special Clocks

This clock was one of the two clocks selected to represent Ferranti at the Royal Academy Exhibition of British Art in Industry, in 1935

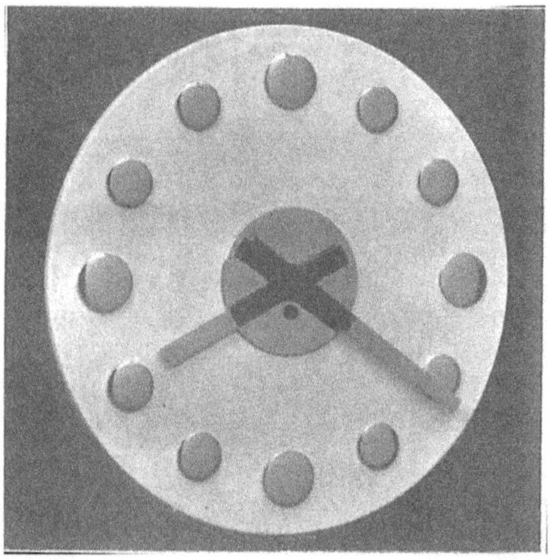

A built in Wall Clock - Wedgwood Blue and Chrome

The Ferranti Flange Clock

All images are courtesy of MOSI

1934

LIST No. C10.

LIST OF FERRANTI SYNCHRONOUS ELECTRIC CLOCKS.

Model No.	Price.	Height.	Width.	Depth.	Page.	Model No.	Price.	Height.	Width.	Depth.	Page.
1	30/–	$6\frac{3}{4}$″	5″	$2\frac{3}{4}$″	4	73	72/–	$5\frac{3}{8}$″	$10\frac{1}{8}$″	$3\frac{1}{4}$″	11
2	30/–	$5\frac{1}{8}$″	$6\frac{3}{4}$″	$2\frac{5}{16}$″	4	75	70/–	$8\frac{1}{4}$″	$9\frac{3}{8}$″	$5\frac{3}{8}$″	9
3	30/–	$6\frac{1}{8}$″	6″	$2\frac{3}{4}$″	4	76	70/–	$8\frac{1}{4}$″	$9\frac{3}{8}$″	$5\frac{3}{8}$″	9
4	35/–	$5\frac{3}{4}$″	$9\frac{7}{16}$″	$3\frac{1}{8}$″	4	77	55/–	9″	$15\frac{3}{4}$″	$4\frac{3}{4}$″	9
5	35/–	$6\frac{3}{8}$″	7″	$3\frac{5}{8}$″	4	80	30/–	$3\frac{11}{16}$″	dia.	$3\frac{3}{8}$″	17
6	25/–	$4\frac{1}{4}$″	$4\frac{1}{4}$″	$2\frac{1}{2}$″	5	81	70/–	$6\frac{3}{8}$″	$8\frac{5}{8}$″	$2\frac{1}{8}$″	12
11	45/–	$4\frac{1}{2}$″	$5\frac{1}{4}$″	$3\frac{3}{8}$″	5	82	72/6	$6\frac{3}{8}$″	$8\frac{5}{8}$″	$3\frac{1}{8}$″	12
12	63/–	$5\frac{7}{8}$″	$4\frac{7}{8}$″	$3\frac{3}{8}$″	5	83	80/–	$6\frac{3}{8}$″	$8\frac{5}{8}$″	$3\frac{1}{8}$″	12
18	£11/0/0	21″ dia	. overall	6″	16	84	90/–	$6\frac{3}{8}$″	$8\frac{5}{8}$″	$3\frac{1}{8}$″	12
19	£7/5/0	$13\frac{1}{2}$″ dia	. overall	6″	16	85	75/–	$8\frac{1}{8}$″	$7\frac{3}{4}$″	$3\frac{1}{8}$″	12
22	65/–	$13\frac{3}{8}$″ dia	. overall	$2\frac{7}{8}$″	16	86	80/–	$8\frac{1}{8}$″	$7\frac{3}{4}$″	$3\frac{1}{8}$″	12
23	57/6	$13\frac{3}{8}$″ dia	. overall	$2\frac{7}{8}$″	16	87	95/–	$8\frac{1}{8}$″	$7\frac{3}{4}$″	$3\frac{1}{8}$″	12
24 Oak	£6/12/6	$17\frac{1}{4}$″	$17\frac{1}{4}$″	$3\frac{1}{8}$″	16	88	70/–	$8\frac{1}{4}$″	$8\frac{3}{8}$″	3″	12
24 Walnut	£7/15/0	$17\frac{1}{4}$″	$17\frac{1}{4}$″	$3\frac{1}{8}$″	16	89	75/–	$8\frac{1}{4}$″	$8\frac{3}{8}$″	3″	12
25	50/–	7″ dia	. overall	$2\frac{7}{8}$″	16	90	90/–	$8\frac{1}{4}$″	$8\frac{3}{8}$″	3″	12
26	97/6	21″ dia	. overall	3″	16	91	67/6	$5\frac{1}{2}$″	$9\frac{5}{8}$″	$3\frac{1}{8}$″	12
27	£7/10/0	21″ dia	. overall	3″	19	92	70/–	$5\frac{1}{2}$″	$9\frac{5}{8}$″	$3\frac{1}{8}$″	12
20	£0/2/6	$11\frac{3}{4}$″	16″	$3\frac{1}{4}$″	17	93	75/–	$5\frac{1}{2}$″	$9\frac{5}{8}$″	$3\frac{1}{8}$″	12
29	£10/15/0	$21\frac{3}{8}$″	16″	$3\frac{1}{4}$″	17	94	80/–	$5\frac{1}{2}$″	$9\frac{5}{8}$″	$0\frac{1}{8}$″	12
30	30/–	$3\frac{11}{16}$″	dia.	$2\frac{3}{4}$″	17	95	67/6	$8\frac{5}{8}$″	$7\frac{15}{16}$″	$2\frac{1}{2}$″	13
31	35/–	$5\frac{1}{2}$″	$10\frac{1}{2}$″	$2\frac{3}{4}$″	5	96	57/6	6″	6″	$2\frac{1}{2}$″	13
32	37/6	$5\frac{3}{4}$″	$10\frac{3}{4}$″	3″	6	97	67/6	$6\frac{5}{8}$″	$9\frac{15}{16}$″	$2\frac{1}{2}$″	13
33	37/6	$5\frac{7}{8}$″	7″	$3\frac{1}{8}$″	6	98	55/–	$4\frac{3}{8}$″	7″	$2\frac{1}{2}$″	13
34	39/–	6″	$9\frac{1}{2}$″	$3\frac{1}{4}$″	6	99	60/–	$6\frac{5}{8}$″	$7\frac{15}{16}$″	$2\frac{1}{2}$″	13
35	40/–	$5\frac{1}{4}$″	$6\frac{1}{2}$″	$3\frac{3}{16}$″	6	100	70/–	$6\frac{5}{8}$″	$7\frac{15}{16}$″	$2\frac{1}{2}$″	13
35a	40/–	$5\frac{1}{4}$″	$6\frac{1}{2}$″	$3\frac{3}{16}$″	6	101	67/6	$6\frac{1}{4}$″	$8\frac{1}{4}$″	$2\frac{5}{8}$″	13
36	42/–	$6\frac{1}{4}$″	9″	$3\frac{1}{2}$″	6	102	52/6	4″	7″	$2\frac{1}{2}$″	13
37	42/–	$5\frac{3}{4}$″	$7\frac{1}{2}$″	$2\frac{3}{4}$″	7	103	57/6	5″	$7\frac{7}{16}$″	$2\frac{1}{2}$″	13
38	42/–	$6\frac{1}{4}$″	$8\frac{3}{4}$″	$2\frac{3}{4}$″	7	104	67/6	5″	$7\frac{7}{16}$″	$2\frac{1}{2}$″	13
39	50/–	$6\frac{1}{4}$″	$8\frac{1}{8}$″	$3\frac{1}{8}$″	7	105	·55/–	$4\frac{5}{8}$″	$7\frac{1}{16}$″	$2\frac{1}{2}$″	13
40	55/–	$5\frac{1}{8}$″	$13\frac{5}{8}$″	$3\frac{1}{8}$″	7	106	65/–	$4\frac{5}{8}$″	$7\frac{1}{16}$″	$2\frac{1}{2}$″	13
41	57/6	6″	$8\frac{1}{2}$″	3″	7	107	52/6	$8\frac{3}{8}$″	$6\frac{3}{8}$″	$2\frac{1}{2}$″	14
41a	63/–	6″	$8\frac{1}{2}$″	3″	8	108	52/6	$6\frac{3}{8}$″	$8\frac{3}{8}$″	$2\frac{1}{2}$″	14
42	57/6	$6\frac{1}{2}$″	$6\frac{7}{8}$″	$3\frac{1}{8}$″	8	109	50/–	$6\frac{3}{8}$″	$6\frac{3}{8}$″	$2\frac{1}{2}$″	14
44	63/–	$5\frac{3}{4}$″	$7\frac{3}{8}$″	$2\frac{3}{4}$″	8	110	50/–	$4\frac{3}{4}$″	$7\frac{3}{8}$″	$2\frac{1}{2}$″	14
50	30/–	$3\frac{11}{16}$″	dia.	$2\frac{3}{4}$″	17	111	45/–	$4\frac{3}{8}$″	$7\frac{3}{8}$″	$2\frac{1}{2}$″	14
51	35/–	$4\frac{3}{4}$″	$8\frac{3}{4}$″	$2\frac{7}{8}$″	8	112	52/6	$5\frac{7}{8}$″	8″	$2\frac{5}{8}$″	14
52	42/–	$4\frac{1}{4}$″	6″	$2\frac{7}{8}$″	8	113	32/6	$4\frac{1}{8}$″	$4\frac{1}{8}$″	$2\frac{3}{4}$″	15
53	50/–	$5\frac{1}{2}$″	$5\frac{3}{4}$″	$2\frac{5}{8}$″	8	114	30/–	$3\frac{11}{16}$″ dia	. overall	$2\frac{1}{4}$″	15
54	57/6	$6\frac{1}{4}$″	$8\frac{1}{8}$″	$3\frac{1}{8}$″	9	115	52/6	8″	6″	$2\frac{1}{2}$″	13
55	63/–	$5\frac{7}{16}$″	$6\frac{9}{16}$″	$2\frac{7}{8}$″	9	116	52/6	6″	8″	$2\frac{1}{2}$″	13
56	84/–	$5\frac{1}{8}$″	$13\frac{5}{8}$″	$3\frac{1}{8}$″	9	117	47/6	6″	6″	$2\frac{1}{2}$″	13
61	84/–	8″	11″	$3\frac{1}{8}$″	10	118	52/6	$5\frac{1}{2}$″	$7\frac{5}{8}$″	$2\frac{5}{8}$″	13
62	95/–	8″	11″	$3\frac{1}{8}$″	10	119	45/–	$4\frac{3}{8}$″	7″	$2\frac{1}{2}$″	13
63	84/–	$9\frac{3}{4}$″	9″	$3\frac{1}{4}$″	10	120	42/6	4″	7″	$2\frac{1}{2}$″	13
64	90/–	$9\frac{3}{4}$″	9″	$3\frac{1}{4}$″	10	121	77/6	$9\frac{1}{2}$″ dia	. overall	$2\frac{7}{8}$″	18
65	84/–	$7\frac{1}{2}$″	$9\frac{1}{2}$″	$3\frac{1}{4}$″	10	122	80/–	$10\frac{3}{8}$″ dia	. overall	$2\frac{7}{8}$″	18
66	90/–	$7\frac{1}{2}$″	$9\frac{1}{2}$″	$3\frac{1}{4}$″	10	123	82/6	$13\frac{3}{8}$″ dia	. overall	$2\frac{7}{8}$″	18
67	90/–	$7\frac{1}{2}$″	$9\frac{1}{2}$″	$3\frac{1}{4}$″	10	124	£11/15/0	17″ dia	. overall	$2\frac{3}{4}$″	18
68	95/–	$7\frac{7}{8}$″	$9\frac{1}{8}$″	$3\frac{1}{8}$″	11	125	£9/0/0	$9\frac{1}{2}$″ dia	. overall	6″	18
69	95/–	$7\frac{3}{8}$″	$9\frac{3}{8}$″	$3\frac{1}{8}$″	11	126	£9/5/0	$10\frac{3}{8}$″ dia	. overall	6″	18
69a	90/–	$7\frac{3}{8}$″	$9\frac{3}{8}$″	$3\frac{1}{8}$″	11	127	£9/10/0	$13\frac{3}{8}$″ dia	. overall	6″	18
70	45/–	6″ dia	. overall	$2\frac{3}{4}$″	17	128	—	$11\frac{1}{4}$″	$11\frac{1}{4}$″	$2\frac{3}{4}$″	18
71	67/6	$5\frac{3}{8}$″	$10\frac{1}{8}$″	$3\frac{1}{4}$″	11	129	—	$13\frac{1}{4}$″	$13\frac{1}{4}$″	$2\frac{3}{4}$″	18
72	70/–	$5\frac{3}{8}$″	$10\frac{1}{8}$″	$3\frac{1}{4}$″	11	200	—	0″ dia	. overall	4″	19

PAGE 20

1936

LIST OF FERRANTI SYNCHRONOUS ELECTRIC CLOCKS

Model No.	Price.	Height.	Width.	Depth.	Page.	Model No.	Price.	Height.	Width.	Depth.	Page.
1	30/–	6¾″	5″	2¾″	4	90	90/–	8⅜″	8⅝″	3″	13
2	30/–	5⅛″	6¾″	2½″	4	91	67/6	5¼″	9¼″	3¼″	13
3	30/–	5⅞″	6″	2¾″	4	92	70/–	5¼″	9¼″	3¼″	13
4	35/–	5¾″	9 7/16″	3⅛″	4	97	52/6	6⅝″	9 15/16″	2½″	15
5	35/–	6⅛″	7″	3⅝″	4	99	50/–	6⅝″	7 15/16″	2½″	15
6	25/–	4¾″	4¼″	2½″	5	103	50/–	5″	7⅝″	2⅜″	15
7	35/–	5¼″	4¼″	2½″	5	105	45/–	4⅝″	6¾″	2⅜″	15
11	45/–	4½″	5¼″	3⅜″	6	107	52/6	8⅜″	6⅜″	2½″	16
12	57/6	5⅛″	4¾″	3⅜″	6	108	52/6	6⅜″	8⅜″	2½″	16
18	£7/5/0	13½″dia.	overall	6″	19	109	50/–	6⅜″	6⅜″	2½″	16
19	£11/0/0	21″ dia.	overall	6″	19	110	50/–	4¾″	7⅜″	2½″	16
22	57/6	13⅜″dia.	overall	2⅞″	19	111	45/–	4⅜″	7⅜″	2½″	16
24 Oak	£6/12/6	17¼″	17¼″	3⅛″	19	112	52/6	6″	8″	2⅝″	16
24 Walnut	£7/15/0	17¼″	17¼″	3⅛″	19	113	32/6	4⅛″	4⅛″	2¾″	17
25	50/–	7″ dia.	overall	2⅞″	19	114	30/–	3 11/16″dia.	overall	2¾″	17
26	97/6	21″ dia.	overall	3″	19	121	62/6	9½″ dia.	overall	2⅞″	20
30	30/–	3⅞″ dia.	overall	2¾″	18	122	67/6	11½″dia.	overall	2⅞″	20
31	35/–	5⅝″	10½″	3¼″	6	123	72/6	13⅜″dia.	overall	2⅞″	20
32	37/6	5¾″	10¾″	3⅛″	6	125	£7/15/0	9½″ dia.	overall	6″	20
33	37/6	5⅞″	6¾″	3¼″	6	126	£8/5/0	11½″dia.	overall	6″	20
34	39/–	6″	9½″	3¼″	7	127	£8/17/6	13⅜″dia.	overall	6″	20
35	40/–	5¼″	6½″	3¼″	7	128	£10/10/0	11¼″	11¼″	2¾″	20
35a	40/–	5¼″	6½″	3¼″	7	129	£13/0/0	13¼″	13¼″	2¾″	20
36	42/–	5⅞″	9″	3½″	7	130	37/6	5¾″	8¼″	3¼″	10
37	42/–	5⅞″	7¼″	3¼″	7	131	37/6	6⅛″	8¼″	3¼″	10
38	42/–	6⅛″	9″	3¼″	8	132	40/–	5¾″	9½″	3¼″	10
38a	49/6	6⅛″	9″	3¼″	8	133	84/–	7⅛″	11⅛″	3½″	12
39	50/–	5½″	7⅞″	3¼″	8	134	90/–	7⅛″	11⅛″	3½″	12
40	55/–	5¼″	13⅝″	3¼″	7	135	92/6	6⅞″	12⅛″	3½″	12
41	57/6	5⅞″	8½″	3¼″	8	136	85/–	7½″	8⅛″	3¼″	12
41a	63/–	5⅞″	8½″	3¼″	8	137	90/–	7½″	8⅛″	3¼″	12
44	63/–	6″	7″	3¼″	8	138	92/6	8″	11″	3¼″	12
50	30/–	3 11/16″	dia.	2¾″	18	150	99/6	54″	10½″	8″	14
50a	32/6	3 11/16″	dia.	2¾″	18	151	195/–	56″	12″	8¾″	14
51	35/–	5″	8¾″	3¼″	9	200	—	8″ dia.	overall	4″	23
53	50/–	5⅝″	5¾″	3¼″	9	201	£6/17/6	24½″dia.	overall	6½″	21
54	57/6	5½″	7⅞″	3⅜″	9	202	£13/17/6	24½″dia.	overall	6½″	21
55	63/–	5½″	6½″	3″	9	203	£7/17/6	30½″dia.	overall	7″	21
56	84/–	5¼″	13⅝″	3¼″	9	204	£15/10/0	30½″dia.	overall	7″	21
61	84/–	8″	11″	3¼″	11	205	£15/15/0	24½″	32″	12½″	21
62	95/–	8″	11″	3¼″	11	206	£18/18/0	24½″	32″	12½″	21
63	84/–	9¾″	9″	3¼″	11	207	£18/0/0	30½″	39½″	12½″	21
64	90/–	9¾″	9″	3¼″	11	208	£21/0/0	30½″	39½″	12½″	21
68	95/–	7⅞″	9⅛″	3¼″	11	209	£22/17/6	23″	32½″	10⅝″	22
69	95/–	7⅜″	9⅜″	3¼″	11	210	£23/0/0	29″	48½″	10⅝″	22
70	45/–	6″ dia.	overall	2¾″	18	211	£6/17/6	23″	23″	7″	22
71	67/6	5⅜″	10⅛″	3¼″	13	212	£13/17/6	23″	23″	7″	22
72	70/–	5¾″	10⅛″	3¼″	13	213	£7/17/6	29″	29″	9″	22
75	70/–	8¼″	9⅜″	5⅜″	10	214	£15/10/0	29″	29″	9″	22
76	70/–	8¼″	9⅜″	5⅜″	10	215	£24/17/6	23″	31″	10⅝″	22
77	55/–	9″	16″	5″	10	216	£28/0/0	29″	37″	10⅝″	22
80	30/–	3 11/16″	dia.	3″	18	217	£8/10/0	20″	22″	3″	23
85	75/–	8⅜″	7¾″	3¼″	13	218	£10/10/0	20″	36″	3″	23
87	95/–	8⅜″	7¾″	3¼″	13	219	£12/0/0	25″	25″	4″	23
88	70/–	8⅜″	8⅝″	3″	13	220	£17/17/0	31″	31″	5½″	23
89	75/–	8⅜″	8⅝″	3″	13						

1950

Ferranti Electric Clocks

PRICE LIST

Model No.	Price	Purchase Tax	Dimensions		
			Height	Width	Depth
12	40/-	8/10	5 3/16"	5 5/16"	2 3/4"
14	50/-	11/-	6 3/4"	8 1/4"	3 1/16"
15	50/-	11/-	6 11/16"	7 1/4"	3 1/16"
16	40/-	8/10	5 5/16"	5"	2 3/4"
17	40/-	8/10	5 11/16"	6 1/8"	2 11/16"
20	85/-	18/8	10 1/4" *		3"
21	90/-	19/10	12 1/8" *		3"
22	95/-	20/11	14 1/8" *		3"
26	175/-	38/6	20 3/4" *		2 15/16"
28	47/6	10/5	8" *		2 7/16"
33	47/6	10/5	5 3/4"	7"	3 3/16"
45	52/6	11/7	5 1/8"	7"	3 3/16"
115	120/-	26/5	7"	8 9/16"	2 3/4"
130	52/6	11/7	5 13/16"	7 7/8"	3 3/16"
132	52/6	11/7	5 11/16"	9 5/16"	3 3/16"
161	47/6	10/6	5 1/2"	7 11/16"	3 5/16"
169	80/-	17/8	7"	8 7/16"	3 13/16"
189	100/-	22/-	11"	11"	2 1/2"
290	57/6	12/8	5 7/8"	5 7/8"	3 1/2"
292	84/-	18/6	6 11/16"	6 3/16"	3 1/4"
293	75/-	16/6	5 13/16"	6 3/4"	3 1/8"
294	84/-	18/6	6 3/8"	6 7/8"	3 1/8"
295	63/-	13/11	5 5/8"	5"	3 1/4"
296	63/-	13/11	5 5/8"	5"	3 1/4"
297	63/-	13/11	5 3/16"	8 3/4"	3 1/8"
299	130/-	28/8	6 1/2"	8 13/16"	3 3/8"
300	47/6	10/6	5 7/16"	7 9/16"	3 5/16"
301	47/6	10/6	5 3/16"	7 7/16"	3 3/8"
303	47/6	10/6	5 1/8"	7 3/8"	3 1/4"
310	52/6	11/7	5 15/16"	8"	3 1/4"
311	52/6	11/7	5 7/8"	7 1/8"	3 3/16"
317	85/-	18/9	8"	11"	4 1/8"
320	90/-	19/10	8 1/8"	9 3/4"	3 13/16"
321	100/-	22/-	8"	6 1/2"	3 13/16"
322	112/6	24/9	7 3/4"	8"	3 7/16"
323	120/-	26/5	8 5/16"	9 9/16"	3 11/16"
324	112/6	24/9	7 1/2"	10 7/8"	3 11/16"
331	47/6	10/6	5 3/4"	5 7/8"	3 3/16"
335	52/-	11/7	5 5/16"	7"	3 3/16"
336	52/6	11/7	6"	7"	3 3/16"
400	65/-	14/4	5 13/16"	6 1/8"	3 9/16"
401	65/-	14/4	6 11/16"	8 1/4"	3 9/16"
402	65/-	14/4	6 3/4"	6 1/8"	4 3/8"
403	65/-	14/4	6 9/16"	8 7/8"	3 1/2"
947	48/9	10/9	4 15/16"	4 1/8"	2 9/16"

*—Diameter

1st FEBRUARY, 1950

DOUBLE SIDED SUSPENSION CLOCKS

Model No. 18. 12" Double Sided Suspension Clock, for interior use.
List Price 263/6d. plus purchase tax 58/-.

Model No. 19. 18" Double Sided Suspension Clock, for interior use.
List Price 369/6d. plus purchase tax 81/4d.

1952

Ferranti Electric Clocks

PRICE LIST

Model No.	Price	Purchase Tax	Dimensions		
			Height	Width	Depth
12	40/–	9/3	5¼″	5¼″	2¾″
14	50/–	11/6	6¾″	8¼″	3″
15	50/–	11/6	6¾″	7¼″	3″
16	40/–	9/3	5¼″	5″	2¾″
17	40/–	9/3	5¾″	6⅛″	2¾″
20	93/–	21/5	10¼″*		3″
21	108/–	24/10	12⅛″*		3″
22	113/–	26/–	14⅛″*		3″
26	197/–	45/4	20¾″*		2¾″
28	50/–	11/6	8″*		2½″
33	47/6	10/11	5¾″	7″	3¼″
45	52/6	12/1	5½″	7″	3¼″
115	120/–	26/5	7″	8½″	2¾″
130	52/6	12/1	5¾″	7⅞″	3¼″
132	52/6	12/1	5¾″	9¼″	3¼″
161	47/6	10/11	5½″	7¾″	3¼″
169	80/–	17/8	7″	8½″	3¾″
189	105/–	24/2	11″	11″	2½″
290	45/–	10/5	5⅞″	5⅞″	3½″
292	84/–	18/6	6¾″	6¼″	3¼″
293	75/–	16/6	5¾″	6¾″	3⅛″
294	84/–	18/6	6⅜″	6⅞″	3⅛″
295	50/–	11/6	5⅝″	5″	3¼″
296	50/–	11/6	5⅝″	5″	3¼″
297	50/–	11/6	5¼″	8¾″	3⅛″
299	130/–	28/8	6½″	8¾″	3⅜″
300	47/6	10/11	5½″	7½″	3¼″
301	47/6	10/11	5¼″	7½″	3⅜″
303	47/6	10/11	5⅛″	7⅜″	3¼″
310	52/6	12/1	6″	8″	3¼″
311	52/6	12/1	5⅞″	7⅛″	3¼″
317	85/–	18/9	8″	11″	4⅛″
320	90/–	19/10	8⅛″	9¾″	3¾″
321	100/–	22/–	8″	6½″	3¾″
322	112/6	24/9	7¾″	8″	3½″
323	120/–	26/5	8¼″	9½″	3¾″
324	112/6	24/9	7½″	10⅞″	3¾″
331	47/6	10/11	5¾″	5⅞″	3¼″
335	52/6	12/1	5¼″	7″	3¼″
336	52/6	12/1	6″	7″	3¼″
400	65/–	14/11	5¾″	6⅛″	3½″
401	65/–	14/11	6¾″	8¼″	3½″
402	65/–	14/11	6¾″	6⅛″	4⅜″
403	65/–	14/11	6½″	8⅞″	3½″
947	37/6	8/8	5″	4⅛″	2½″

*—Diameter

1st FEBRUARY, 1952

DOUBLE SIDED SUSPENSION CLOCKS

Model No. 18. 12″ Double Sided Suspension Clock, for interior use. List Price 263/6d. plus purchase tax 58/–.

Model No. 19. 18″ Double Sided Suspension Clock, for interior use. List Price 369/6d. plus purchase tax 81/4d.

1955

PRICE

FERRANTI ELECTRIC CLOCKS

LIST

Model No.	*Price*	*Purchase Tax*	*Dimensions*		
			Height	*Width*	*Depth*
			in.	in.	in.
20	100/–	17/3	$10\frac{1}{4}$*		3
21	115/6	19/11	$12\frac{1}{8}$*		3
22	122/6	21/2	$14\frac{1}{8}$*		3
26	212/6	36/8	$20\frac{3}{4}$*		$2\frac{3}{4}$
28	50/–	8/8	8*		$2\frac{1}{2}$
115	120/–	19/10	7	$8\frac{1}{2}$	$2\frac{3}{4}$
189	113/–	19/6	11	11	$2\frac{1}{2}$
290	45/–	7/9	$5\frac{7}{8}$	$5\frac{7}{8}$	$3\frac{1}{2}$
295	50/–	8/8	$5\frac{5}{8}$	5	$3\frac{1}{4}$
296	50/–	8/8	$5\frac{5}{8}$	5	$3\frac{1}{4}$
297	50/–	8/8	$5\frac{1}{4}$	$8\frac{3}{4}$	$3\frac{1}{8}$
299	130/–	21/5	$6\frac{1}{2}$	$8\frac{3}{4}$	$3\frac{3}{8}$
400	65/–	11/3	$5\frac{3}{4}$	$6\frac{1}{8}$	$3\frac{1}{2}$
401	65/–	11/3	$6\frac{3}{4}$	$8\frac{1}{4}$	$3\frac{1}{2}$
402	65/–	11/3	$6\frac{3}{4}$	$6\frac{1}{8}$	$4\frac{3}{8}$
403	65/–	11/3	$6\frac{1}{2}$	$8\frac{7}{8}$	$3\frac{1}{2}$
551	60/–	10/4	$5\frac{5}{8}$	$6\frac{1}{2}$	3
552	99/–	16/5	$6\frac{5}{8}$	6	3
553	99/–	16/5	$6\frac{1}{8}$	$7\frac{1}{2}$	3
554	70/–	11/7	7	9	3
555	75/–	12/5	7	8	3
556	84/–	13/10	$6\frac{3}{8}$	$8\frac{5}{8}$	$3\frac{3}{8}$

* Diameter.

DOUBLE-SIDED SUSPENSION CLOCKS

Model No. 18 12 in. Double-sided Suspension Clock, for interior use. List Price 283/– plus purchase tax 48/10.

Model No. 19 18 in. Double-sided Suspension Clock, for interior use. List Price 435/– plus purchase tax 75/–.

FERRANTI LTD
DOMESTIC APPLIANCE SALES, MOSTON, MANCHESTER 10
September 1955

Clock model numbers by date

Early 1932	Late 1932	June, 1933	1934-1935	1936	1938	1947	1950	1952	1955	
1	1	1	1	1						**Bakelite clocks**
2	2	2	2	2						
3	3	3	3	3	3					
4	4	4	4	4						
5	5	5	5	5	5					
			6	6						
				7	7					alarm
				8	8	8				
					9					alarm
						10				
	11	11	11	11	11	11				
						12	12	12		
							14	14		
							15	15		
						16	16	16		
						17	17	17		
									551	Polystyrene - alarm
						947	947	947		alarm
	31	31	31	31						**3.5 inch dial mantel clocks**
	32	32	32	32						
	33	33	33	33	33	33	33	33		
	34	34	34	34						
	35	35	35	35						
		35a	35a	35a						
	36	36	36	36						
	37	37	37	37						
	38	38	38	38						
			38a	38a	38a					
	39	39	39	39						
	40	40	40	40						
	41	41	41	41						
			41a	41a						
	42	42	42	42						
	43									
	44	44	44							
					45	45	45	45		
					46					
					47					
			51	51						
			52	52						
			53	53						
			54	54	54					
			55							
					57					
					58					
					59					
				130	130	130	130	130		
				131	131					
				132	132	132	132	132		
					160					
					161	161	161	161		
					162					
					163					
					164					
					165					
					253					
					254					
						300	300	300		
						301	301	301		
						303	303	303		
						310	310	310		
						311	311	311		
						330				
						331	331	331		
						332				
						335	335	335		
						336	336	336		

Clock model numbers by date

Early 1932	Late 1932	June, 1933	1934-1935	1936	1938	1947	1950	1952	1955	
						400	400	400	400	**4.5 inch dial**
						401	401	401	401	
						402	402	402	402	
						403	403	403	403	
					166					**5 inch dial mantel clocks**
					167					
					168					
					169	169	169	169		
					170	170				
					246					
					247					
					248					
									554	
									555	
									556	
			61							**6 inch dial mantel clocks**
			62							
		75	75	75						
		76	76	76						
			77	77						
				115	115	115	115	115	115	Chrome
					171					
					172					
					173					
					174					
					245					
					251					
					252					
						316				
						317	317	317		
						320	320			
							321	321		
							322	322		
							323	323		
							324	324		
									552	
			56							**shaped dial mantel clocks**
			65							
			66							
			67							
			71	71						
			72	72						
			73							
			81							
			82							
			83							
			84							
			88	88						
			89	89						
			90	90						
			91	91	91					
			92	92	92					
			93	93	93					
			94	94	94					
				133	133					
				134	134					
				135						
					175					
					176					
			85	85	85					**6 inch square dial mantel clocks**
			86							
			87	87	87					
				136	136					
				137	137					
				140	140					
				141	141					
						320		320		

Clock model numbers by date

Early 1932	Late 1932	June, 1933	1934-1935	1936	1938	1947	1950	1952	1955	
			61	61	61					**8x6 inch rectangular dials**
			62	62	62					
			68	68						
				138						
				139	139					
				142	142					
				143	143					
					191					
			63	63						**6x8 inch rectangular dials**
			64	64						
			69	69						
			69a							
					177					
					178					
					179					
				144	144					**Striking and chiming clocks**
				145	145					
				146	146					no seconds hands on these models
				147	147					
				148	148					
				149	149					chime
					180					
					181					
					182					
					185					chime
					186					chime
			95							**Strut clocks**
			96							
			97	97	97					dial change from silver to cream
			98							
			99	99	99					
			100	new 100	new 100					no seconds hand
			101							
			102							
			103	103	103					
			104							
			105	105	105					
			106							
			115	new 115	new 115					
			116		116					
			117							
			118							
			119							
			120							
					104					**Fancy clocks**
					117					
					243	243				
					249					
					250					
						288				
						295	295	295	295	
						296	296	296	296	
					110					**Glass and Chrome**
					118					
					119					
					120					no pic from mosi but in CLKS
					240					
					241					
					242					
					244					
						290	290	290	290	
						292	292	292		
						293	293	293		
						294	294	294		
						297	297	297	297	
							299	299	299	
									553	

Clock model numbers by date

Early 1932	Late 1932	June, 1933	1934-1935	1936	1938	1947	1950	1952	1955	
										Flush Fitting
			107	107	107					
			108	108	108					
			109	109	109					
			110	110	110					
			111	111	111					
			112	112	112					
			113	113	113					ball and socket fixing
			114	114	114					ball and socket fixing
			128	128	128					
			129	129	129					
				150	150					**Grand-Daughter Clocks**
				151	151					
					152					
					153					
										Wall Clocks
			18	18	18			18	18	double sided
			19	19	19			19	19	double sided
					20	20	20	20	20	
					21	21	21	21	21	
	22	22	22	22	22	22	22	22	22	
	23	23	23							
	24	24	24	24	24					oak
			24a	24a	24a					
			25	25						
			26	26	26	26	26	26	26	
			27	27	27	27				bakelite
	28	28	28	28	20	28	28	28	28	
	29	29	29	29	29					bakelite
			121	121	121					
			122	122	122					
			123	123	123					
			124							
			125	125	125					double sided
			126	126	126					double sided
			127	127	127					double sided
					187					
					188					
					189	189	189	189	189	
					190					
				201	201					**Outdoor Clocks**
				202	202					
				203	203					
				204	204					
				205	205					**Double sided- outdoor**
				206	206					
				207	207					
				208	208					
				209	209					
				210	210					
				211	211					
				212	212					
				213	213					
				214	214					
				215	215					
				216	216					
				217						
				218						
				219	219					cinema clock
				220	220					cinema clock
	30	30	30	30	30					**Movements**
					30a					
	50	50	50	50	50					
				50a	50a					
		70	70	70	70					
	80	80	80	80	80					
			200	200						**Stop Clock**

Lightning Source UK Ltd.
Milton Keynes UK
UKHW03n1921170618
324246UK00003B/53/P

9 780957 217218